12/2020

D1400385

BRIDGEWATER PUBLIC LIBRARY
15 SOUTH STREET
BRIDGEWATER, MA 02324

INFLUENTIAL
L!VES

GAL GADOT

ISRAELI ACTOR AND MODEL

Kathy Furgang

Enslow Publishing
101 W. 23rd Street
Suite 240
New York, NY 10011
USA

enslow.com

*For my mother-in-law, Sandy—who has influenced
my life in so many positive ways*

Published in 2019 by Enslow Publishing, LLC.
101 W. 23rd Street, Suite 240, New York, NY 10011

Copyright © 2019 by Enslow Publishing, LLC.

All rights reserved.

No part of this book may be reproduced by any means without the written permission of the publisher.

Library of Congress Cataloging-in-Publication Data
Names: Furgang, Kathy, author.
Title: Gal Gadot : Israeli actor and model / Kathy Furgang.
Description: New York : Enslow Publishing, [2019] | Series: Influential lives
| Audience: Grades 7-12. | Includes bibliographical references and index.
Identifiers: LCCN 2018010348| ISBN 9781978503410 (library bound) | ISBN
9781978505162 (pbk.)
Subjects: LCSH: Gadot, Gal, 1985- | Actresses—Israel—Biography. | Jewish
actors—Israel—Biography.
Classification: LCC PN2919.8.G33 F87 2018 | DDC 791.4302/8092 [B] —dc23
LC record available at https://lccn.loc.gov/2018010348

Printed in the United States of America

To Our Readers: We have done our best to make sure all websites in this book were active and appropriate when we went to press. However, the author and the publisher have no control over and assume no liability for the material available on those websites or on any websites they may link to. Any comments or suggestions can be sent by e-mail to customerservice@enslow.com.

Photo credits: Cover, pp. 1, 89 Kathy Hutchins/Shutterstock.com; pp. 4, 92 Vera Anderson/WireImage/Getty Images; p. 9 Arkadiy Yarmolenko/Shutterstock.com; p. 13 ullstein bild/Getty Images; p. 16 AFP/Getty Images; p. 20 Getty Images; p. 23 Ray Tamarra/Getty Images; p. 24 Marwan Naamani/AFP/Getty Images; pp. 28, 39, 73 Moviestore collection Ltd/Alamy Stock Photo; p. 31 Everett Collection, Inc./Alamy Stock Photo; p. 35 Pictorial Press Ltd/Alamy Stock Photo; p. 37 © AP Images; pp. 43, 82 Entertainment Pictures/Alamy Stock Photo; pp. 45, 48 Clay Enos/© Warner Bros. Pictures/Courtesy Everett Collection; p. 54 Gabe Ginsberg/Getty Images; p. 59 Keith Homan/Alamy Stock Photo; p. 61 Silver Screen Collection/Moviepix/Getty Images; p. 65 Mike Coppola/Getty Images; p. 68 Collection Christophel/Alamy Stock Photo; pp. 77, 95 Mike Coppola/WireImage/Getty Images; p. 79 Jordan Strauss/Invision/AP; p. 85 Josiah Kamau/BuzzFoto/Getty Images; p. 101 Frazer Harrison/Getty Images; p. 103 Evan Agostini/Invision/AP; p. 104 s_bukley/Shutterstock.com; back cover and interior pages background graphic zffoto/Shutterstock.com.

Contents

Introduction

······························

When the DC superhero film *Wonder Woman* opened across the United States in June of 2017, Warner Brothers and DC Comics had high hopes for the movie's success. Little did they know that the film would exceed all of their expectations, with $100.5 million in box office earnings on its opening weekend alone. Combined with the other openings around the world, the movie had the third largest opening weekend for DC Comics.

The story of Diana Prince as Wonder Woman captivated audiences. But was the success of the film due only to the story and appeal of the female superhero? The breakout performance of actress Gal Gadot as Diana Prince definitely contributed to the film's success.

By the end of 2017, Gadot was the highest grossing actress of the year. Her starring role brought $1.4 billion

Gal Gadot has become a household name thanks to her star-making performance as superhero Wonder Woman.

in movie ticket sales. According to *Forbes* magazine, *Wonder Woman* was the highest earning superhero origin movie of all time. People all around the world were inspired by the strong-willed hero always battling for justice, sometimes referred to as a peaceful warrior. Just as the superhero Wonder Woman has been a feminist icon since she was invented by DC in 1941, actress Gal Gadot seems to have filled that role in real life.

The Israeli-born actress spent years as a combat trainer for the armed forces. Her experience helped give her the discipline and strength needed for such a physically demanding role.

Her rise as an actress even mirrored the struggle many women face in the working world. To introduce the character of Wonder Woman to an already popular DC Extended Universe of films, Warner Brothers hired Gadot for a three-movie contract. She would earn $300,000 for each film, a salary much lower than many of her male counterparts. While her first role, in 2016's *Batman v. Superman: Dawn of Justice*, was relatively small, her second film in the contract, *Wonder Woman*, was a starring role. Gadot proved herself so strongly in that film that she was able to negotiate her next contract with much more success. She was even able to negotiate the dismissal of a producer involved in claims of sexual misconduct.

The Wonder Woman franchise is a success in large part due to the actress who plays the part, Gal Gadot. Since the 1940s, the superhero has been a part of the DC Universe, along with Batman, Superman, the Flash, and Green Lantern. But director Patty Jenkins's interpretation of Wonder Woman on-screen depicts a hero that everyday people can identify with and aspire to.

Since the release of *Wonder Woman*, there has been a surge of female superheroes in film. Gadot's character has even made rival superhero universe Marvel take notice. To compete with the successful DC franchise, actress Brie Larson was introduced as Captain Marvel in 2018.

Gal Gadot's career and professional contributions have taken off as well. She has been a role model for women and girls around the world, and her career has only just begun.

CHAPTER ONE

Girlhood

· · · · · · · · · · · ·

G al Gadot was born on April 30, 1985, in the Israeli city of Rosh HaAyin, just outside Tel Aviv. Gadot's mother, Irit, is a physical education teacher, and her father, Michael, was a mechanical engineer. She has a younger sister, Dana. "Gadot" is a family name chosen by her parents. As Gadot told talk show host Jimmy Kimmel in an interview in 2016, her name was originally Greenstein. Her parents chose the last name Gadot, which means "riverbank" in Hebrew. Gadot's first name, Gal, means "wave."

As children, Gal and her sister were encouraged to play outside a lot. In an interview with *Rolling Stone* magazine, Gadot talked about her physically active youth. "I had a very sheltered kind of life. There was no TV-watching. It was always 'Take a ball and go play.' In general, I was a good girl, a good student, a pleaser, and I was a tomboy. Always with wounds and scratches on my

Gadot was born in Israel in the rural settlement of Rosh HaAyin.
The name means "fountainhead" and seemed fitting because of
the settlement's location at the source of the Yarkon River.

knees."[1] She enjoyed athletics, such as volleyball, tennis, and basketball.

In addition to her love of sports, Gadot had a strong love of dance. When she was young, she thought she might want to grow up to be a choreographer.

In some ways, a childhood in Israel is similar to life in the United States. The city where Gadot grew up had many of the same companies and corporations that can be found in America. For instance, Gadot worked at a Burger King as her first job in high school. However, Israel is different than the United States in many ways, too. Nearly all Israeli citizens over the age of eighteen are required to serve in the armed forces. One of the few exceptions is Arab citizens. Gadot left her job at Burger

How Do You Pronounce That?

Gal Gadot's name is one of the most mispronounced names in Hollywood. The name is often mistaken for French, and in that language a *t* at the end of a word is usually not pronounced. So, people frequently mispronounce her name as *Ga-dough*. However, the family name is pronounced *Guh-dot*, with a hard *t* sound. In 2017, Gal Gadot appeared on *Jimmy Kimmel Live* and demonstrated how to pronounce the name correctly. News organization CNN included Gadot's name in an article called "2017: The Year Americans Couldn't Say Gal Gadot (and a Lot of Other Words)." The name "Gadot" was included along with the Caribbean island of Puerto Rico and the capital of North Korea, Pyongyang.

King to serve in the Israel Defense Forces (IDF), an experience that helped shape the rest of her life.

A Family History

Gal Gadot's family originated in Europe before the creation of the nation of Israel. Like many Jewish families in Europe during World War II, they felt the damaging impact of Adolf Hitler's Nazi forces. The war, which took place between 1939 and 1945, was fought largely in Europe and Japan. One of the main reasons for the war was that Hitler wanted to expand Germany far beyond its borders. In addition to the invasions of nearby nations, Hitler considered Jews and some other minority groups "enemies of the state." Camps were set up all around Europe to detain these groups, make them take part in forced labor, and eventually execute them. These camps, called concentration camps, included gas chambers for committing mass murders on large numbers of people using poisonous gases. One of the largest concentration camps—and the one most famously known today because of the horrors committed within it—is Auschwitz, in Poland. This single complex was responsible for the death of a million people during the war. The war itself contributed to the extermination of up to six million Jews, a devastating number from which the faith has yet to recover.

During this Holocaust, entire families were moved to ghettos, shipped to camps, forced into labor, and executed. To fight this and other massive human rights violations going on at the time, war broke out between the collective forces of Nazi Germany, Japan, and Italy, known as the Axis powers, and the opposing Allied powers. The Allies in the war included Great Britain, France, China, the United States, and the Soviet Union. The war was one of the most devastating in history, killing millions of people and creating massive destruction in many of Europe's most culturally historic cities.

Gal Gadot's family was affected directly by the war. Gadot's grandfather—her mother's dad—experienced great hardships from the war. Abraham Weiss was thirteen years old when Nazis invaded his Czechoslovakian village of Munkács. The young boy saw his father go into the army and not return. He was sent away with the rest of his family to the concentration camp Auschwitz. His mother and brother were killed in the gas chambers there.

When the war ended, the boy made his way by himself to the newly formed nation of Israel. As an agreement at the end of the war, the State of Israel was formed in 1948 for the displaced Jews of the war. Israel was formed in Palestine, an Arab region in the Middle East. Israel was recognized as a new nation by the United States. It was meant to be a place where Jews who survived the war, such as Gal Gadot's grandfather, could go and start a new life. Gadot's family has lived there ever since.

When Israel was first established in 1948, it had just over 800,000 residents. Today, it has well over 8 million residents. Israel's population is still about 75 percent Jewish, but it does have an Arab population of about 20 percent.[2] Because of its location amid a largely Arab region, the nation has not been recognized by all of its Middle Eastern neighbors. As a result, Israel

David Ben-Gurion declared independence of the state of Israel on May 14, 1948. He also served as Israel's first prime minister, a post he held until 1963, with one brief interruption.

> **"He always told me if you forget about your history, the history will repeat itself."**

has developed a strong military, and it has been involved in many confrontations in the decades since it was established—especially with the Palestinian population that shares some of the land under its designated control. The political disputes that Israel experiences over borders and other issues in the Middle East are one of the reasons it requires all its citizens to have military training.

Gal Gadot is proud of her Jewish heritage. She told an Israeli website, "I definitely have a strong sense of my Jewish and Israeli identity. I was brought up in a very Jewish, Israeli family environment, so of course my heritage is very important to me. I want people to have a good impression of Israel. I find that people in the US,

Ashkenazi Jewish Culture

Gal Gadot's family belongs to a division of the Jewish faith called Ashkenazi Jews. This group originated in eastern Europe and can be traced back thousands of years to a group of less than five hundred people. Modern Ashkenazi Jews include mathematician Albert Einstein, film director Steven Spielberg, actress Scarlett Johansson, and US Supreme Court justices Ruth Bader Ginsburg and Elena Kagan.

especially in Hollywood, tend to have positive opinions on Israel—both Jewish and non-Jewish people alike."[3]

In a 2017 interview with *Elle* magazine, Gadot discussed the importance of her grandfather's story and her sense of responsibility to teach others about that time in history. "One of the stories I'm developing is about the Holocaust from a woman's perspective. I feel like this is part of my mission, to tell the story, because it was such a horror." Her grandfather, Abraham Weiss, passed away in 2014. She explained, "He always told me if you forget about your history, the history will repeat itself."[4]

A Model Beginning

The Gadot family has always been supportive of Gal and her interests. In fact, her mother and sister, Dana, signed Gadot up for the 2004 Miss Israel beauty pageant without her knowledge. They knew the pageant would be something Gadot would not pursue on her own, but they believed that she could be a serious contender for the title.

The eighteen-year-old Gadot was on her year off between high school and college, so she had time to enter the competition when it accepted her. She later told *Rolling Stone* magazine, "I told myself, 'I'm just gonna do this. They're gonna fly us to Europe, and I'm gonna get to tell my grandchildren that Grandmom did the Miss Israel thing.' Little did I know that I would win."[5] During the competition, Gadot performed the Hebrew version of the 1980 Irene Cara hit song, "Fame." When she was finally the last contestant standing, she won the pageant crown as well as a car—a Citroën C3 supermini.

After winning the title of Miss Israel, Gadot appeared in the Miss Universe pageant in 2004. Eighty contestants from nations around the world participated in the event.

Because Gadot did not compete prior to the competition and she had not entered the competition of her own accord, she was not aware of all of the rules. She didn't realize that her victory in the Miss Israel contest made her an automatic contestant to represent Israel in the Miss Universe pageant of that year.

That's where Gadot's interest stopped. She felt that the title would mean too much responsibility for her, still in her teenage years. She decided to do the only thing that would get her out of the responsibility of being Miss Universe—she lost the competition on purpose.

While the Miss Israel pageant was held in the Hebrew language, Miss Universe contestants were expected to know English. Gadot pretended that she could not speak English, making her chances of winning much less. She even wore the wrong clothing for different sections of the contest to ensure her loss. In an interview with *People* magazine about the experience, Gadot reported,

> I really didn't want to win the Miss Universe pageant. It was too much being Miss Israel. I was 19. I wasn't that type of girl. I rebelled. I came down late. I showed up late to everything. They make you wear evening gowns for breakfast. I didn't wear evening gowns to breakfast. I didn't wear my makeup. I remember Paula Abdul was part of the judges and she was asking me a question and I just said I don't understand. And I successfully didn't win.[6]

She took some parts of the contest seriously, however, knowing that she was representing her country. As she walked the stage wearing her swimsuit and evening gowns in the competition, an announcer read prepared materials about Gadot based on her ideals. They were translated into different languages for the audience. The details read, "She is intent on keeping her principles and always making her own decisions in life." Another quotation stated, "Miss Israel calls herself a very social person. She believes that having many solid relationships and a variety of friends makes life more interesting and fruitful."[7]

Gadot's efforts at losing paid off, however, and she did not even make it into the top 20 finalist category. As she told *Rolling Stone* about the experience, "I lost majorly. I victoriously lost."[8]

While her experiences as a beauty queen were not entirely positive, they helped her to realize what she *did* want to do. She knew she loved to perform, and she knew that she loved dance and athletics. The next stages in her life helped to lead her to be the influence she is today for countless young girls around the world.

CHAPTER TWO

To Protect, Serve, and Grow

· · · · · · · · · · · · · ·

G rowing up in Israel provides a different experience for children than growing up in the United States. The youth there are no strangers to the political struggles of their government. As Gal Gadot grew up in the city of Rosh HaAyin, she knew that she would have to go into the Israeli Defense Forces for two years, just like all of the other Jewish friends she grew up with.

Israel is the only country in the world that requires military service for women. Since the country's beginning, the idea was that women should share the duties of protecting the nation. David Ben-Gurion, Israel's first prime minister, was also the country's first defense minister. He said about the service of women in Israel's army, "The Army is the supreme symbol of duty, and as long as women are not equal to men in performing this duty, they have not yet obtained true equality. If the daughters of Israel are absent from the army, then the

As part of their training for the Israeli Defense Forces, these women learn to camouflage themselves with mud and branches. After more than two months of training, the women then train others.

● ●

character of the Yishuv [Jewish community in Israel] will be distorted."[1]

Israeli youth grow up knowing to expect the two years of service. The military sees the service not only as a way to defend the country, but a way to integrate society. People from all social and economic backgrounds meet up for their training in the IDF. Where eighteen-year-olds in other nations are often leaving home to go to a university, the IDF training is the common experience for Israeli youth.

Gadot explained her support for the idea of serving her country in a 2016 interview with the *Jakarta Post*. She said,

Let me start by saying that I wish no country would ever need an army. Unfortunately, it's not the case in Israel, and for me, it's just so normal. My parents went to the Army, my grandparents went to the Army, and my friends went to the Army. My best friend is a fighter pilot; it's the reality of Israel. When you reach 18, you have to do the service. It's hard, because you have to give up your freedom for two years, but on the other hand, there is something beautiful about giving back to the community, and that is our way to give back to our country.[2]

From Boot Camp to Combat Trainer

Gadot's three-month experience at boot camp in the Israeli Defense Forces started in 2005, when she was

A Well-Equipped Military

The IDF was not always as well equipped as it is today. When the defense forces first began during Israel's founding in 1948, its resources were very slim. Into the 1950s even most senior commanders did not earn pay for their services and had to live by growing their own food. Today, the army is one of the strongest in the world. The IDF has developed high-tech weapon systems able to shoot down rockets carrying warheads. According to *Business Insider,* the IDF has a $17-billion budget, 160,000 active soldiers, more than 4,000 tanks, and close to 700 aircraft vehicles. In addition to these resources, the nation has nuclear weapons and makes use of the newest technologies, including drones and satellites.[3]

twenty years old. She had already won the Miss Israel title and had competed in the Miss Universe pageant a year earlier.

Similar to the experiences in any military training boot camp, Gadot was trained extensively in physical fitness, weapons, and preparation for different combat situations. Military trainees typically wake up very early in the morning and do difficult exercises, and they must listen to their commanders and perform to the best of their ability. According to an IDF volunteer informational website, "Every recruit goes through a basic training program where they are taught the basics of army discipline, shooting, first aid, information on chemical and biological warfare and physical fitness."[4]

The physical drills, eating and sleeping, and weapons and other educational training are all done in groups with other soldiers. These group situations form a bond between the soldiers and train them for possible future situations when they may have to work as a team and cooperate on military missions or other situations of war.

A soldier's training also includes lessons in leadership and teamwork that can be used in a career in the military or later in the trainee's professional life outside the armed forces. Recruits may be trained in computer programming, engineering, or other areas such as teaching.

Like all other recruits, Gadot first received basic training. Then she received her assignment for serving, which allowed her to specialize and offer her skills to others. She was assigned to be a trainer to other soldiers to keep them physically fit.

Gadot attended a 2007 celebration by *Maxim* magazine of "Women of the Israeli Defense Forces." The army training would serve her well in Hollywood.

The Lebanon War, or Israel-Hezbolla War, decimated Lebanese villages like this one. The troubled relations between the two countries led Lebanon to ban Gadot's movie.

After basic training, Gadot was given her assignment as part of her two-year service in the IDF. In a 2016 interview with the *Sydney Morning Herald*, Gadot explained her assignment. "I was a combat instructor. I was never on the field doing anything dangerous or with weapons. I was in the gym training soldiers and keeping them in shape. I did that for two years. I did learn to use a weapon in boot camp.

> **"I taught gymnastics and calisthenics. The soldiers loved me because I made them fit."**

But I was never in a situation where I had to use one."[5] She told *Maxim* in a 2007 interview, "I taught gymnastics and calisthenics. The soldiers loved me because I made them fit."[6]

Gadot's training in the IDF and her work as a combat trainer helped lead to her success in the movies. The roles she landed required both weapons knowledge and physical strength and training, which she learned while serving her native country of Israel.

Wonder Woman Ban

Gadot's military work affected her movie career in more ways than just giving her the skills she learned while training. Her military service caused the nation of Lebanon to actually ban her film *Wonder Woman*.

The history between Lebanon and Israel is a difficult and violent one. During the time that Gadot served in the IDF, a fierce battle between Israel and an extremist

Muslim group called Hezbollah occurred. The group is especially active in Lebanon, and in 2006—one of Gadot's two years as a combat trainer—a thirty-four-day conflict known as the 2006 Lebanon War occurred. The conflict is sometimes known as the Israel-Hezbollah War.

According to Human Rights Watch, the conflict caused "at least 1,109 Lebanese deaths, the vast majority of whom were civilians, 4,300 injured, and an estimated 1 million displaced."[7]

Celebrities Who Served

Gal Gadot is not the only celebrity to have served her country. Other people in the entertainment industry have gone through basic training and served their countries. Some have even served in wars. Celebrity veterans include former professional wrestler and politician Jesse Ventura, who served in the US Navy from 1969 to 1975. Musician Shaggy served as a Marine during Operation Desert Storm, the first Gulf War of the early 1990s. Celebrities in the military also include action film heroes such as Chuck Norris and Clint Eastwood. Eastwood served during the Korean War of the early 1950s, and Norris was stationed in Korea after the war, where he was introduced to the martial arts that made him famous. Even Marvel comic book legend Stan Lee served in the military. The creator of superheroes such as Spiderman and the Incredible Hulk served in the US Army during World War II.

The strained relations between Israel and Lebanon go back far beyond the 2006 Lebanon War. For decades, many Middle Eastern nations, including Lebanon, have refused to recognize Israel as a nation. Some of these mainly-Arab nations, called the Arab League, take part in no diplomatic relations with the country and lead boycotts against it. The Arab League instead supports the Palestinians, who were displaced and no longer recognized when Israel was made a nation. The difficult relations all throughout the Middle East make Israel an isolated nation with few supporters in its physical region.

Just days before *Wonder Woman* was set to be released in Lebanon, the film was banned by the Interior Minister of Lebanon, "based on the recommendation of the Arab League's Israel Boycott Office."[8]

While the boycott did not seem to have a negative effect on the film's blockbuster success around the world, the film's studio did not wish to see a political firestorm associated with the film or its lead actress.

A ban on Gadot's first portrayal as Wonder Woman in *Batman v. Superman: Dawn of Justice* was attempted by the Arab League but was not successful. The ban of *Wonder Woman* was considered a success.

In an Israeli television station interview soon after the opening of the film, Gadot was asked her opinion about Lebanon's ban on the film. Gadot replied to the question and gave her opinion about the situation. However, according to the *Times of Israel,* the film's producers did not want to have political opinions associated with the film's opening. As a result, they asked that the portion

Wonder Woman was a great success when it opened. At the time, it was one of the top-grossing superhero origin films ever released.

of the interview where Gadot speaks about the ban be removed from the segment.

In response to their request, the Israeli television station reported on the censorship and did not air any of the interview. Overall, the ban did not affect the positive response to film, and *Wonder Woman* was received for its overall feminist message rather than any political message about its star. However, the incident did prompt a dialogue between bloggers and political commentators.[9]

According to *Variety* magazine, popular Lebanese blogger Elie Fares mocked the ban as senseless, arguing that in today's digital age, it's nearly impossible to ban popular culture. He objected to his government's action of banning the film because it would still receive recognition and attention through social media. Fares tweeted, "Can you also ban Facebook, WhatsApp, Instagram, Viber, Starbucks, all smartphones, and laptops?"[10]

He also argued on his popular blog that a boycott against *Wonder Woman* would be of no help for the mission of the Arab League. "Resist what? A movie about an iconic superhero who's been part of pop culture for over 70 years. A movie in which the lead actress happens to be Israeli?"[11]

CHAPTER THREE

Hollywood's New Gal

· · · · · · · · · · · · ·

After her time in the Israeli Defense Forces, Gadot returned home to continue her education. At university, she took classes to study international law. The efforts did not last more than a year, however, before she was pulled in another direction. Gadot was approached by an acting director who had flown to Israel from London to audition actresses for a role as a "Bond Girl." The popular spy thriller series about secret service agent James Bond, known as 007, has been made since the early 1960s. Each film features a female character in an important role alongside hero Bond. The opportunity to be a Bond Girl can be an important way to boost an actress's career. Many Bond Girls have gone on to extensive film careers in Hollywood. The role Gadot was encouraged to audition for was Camille Montes in the 2008 film *Quantum of Solace,* the twenty-second film in the famous James Bond franchise.[1]

Gadot had auditioned for a role in the 2008 James Bond film *Quantum of Solace*, but the role ultimately went to Olga Kurylenko. The film stars Daniel Craig as 007.

31

Although she was honored to be considered for the role, Gadot was not interested. She was concerned that her English was not good enough to work on a film written entirely in English and a movie set operating entirely in English. In addition, Gadot did not consider herself an actress. Although she was known for modeling and her tenure as Miss Israel, she was not an actress and did not feel confident going for the role. She was more intent on continuing school and becoming a lawyer. In an interview with *W* magazine, Gadot admitted that she was originally not interested in acting. She had even figured she was "too smart" to become an actress.[2]

Despite her feelings about the audition, she went to it anyway. The young Gadot was unprepared, however. She recalled to *Insider* magazine that she tried to prepare and study for two scenes while she was driving to the audition. When she arrived, she admitted her inexperience to the casting director—an unusual decision for many aspiring actresses, who often inflate their resumes in order to get the job. "I didn't want her to be upset with me for coming and wasting her time not being prepared and me and my broken English."[3]

Gadot didn't fail the audition as she had feared she would. Instead, she was called back for more auditions and camera tests. During those months, Gadot worked with an acting coach and began to change her mind about acting. She became more interested in the craft and considered it much more fun than practicing law. Even though the role eventually went to Ukrainian actress Olga Kurylenko, Gadot was hooked on the idea of pursuing acting further.

She began taking acting classes. After just three months, she landed her first role in an Israeli television show called *Bubot*, which is Hebrew for "babes." She had a costarring role, as Merry Elkayam, in the show about the modeling world. The show lasted two seasons, spanning 2007 and 2008.

After *Bubot,* Gadot had some other small roles. She appeared in an episode of the popular HBO show *Entourage* and costarred in the short-lived television series *The Beautiful Life: TBL,* both in 2009.[4] That year was also the year Gadot's acting career really began to take off, with an opportunity to join the cast of the popular action movie series The Fast and the Furious.

Fast & Furious

Gal Gadot's first role in a highly visible Hollywood film was in 2009's *Fast & Furious.* Gadot played the role of

"Red Leather, Never Yellow Leather"

Gadot's entry into Hollywood movies meant that she had to work on sets where people speak entirely in English and her own English had to improve. Part of her training as an actress was voice and dialogue training. While her deep voice and Israeli accent are part of her trademark, she worked to improve her broken English. According to an interview with *Elle* magazine, part of her dialogue exercises was the phrase "red leather, never yellow leather."[5] The *r, v, w,* and *th* consonant blends allowed her to practice some of the more difficult sounds in the English language.

Gisele Yashar. She worked with director Justin Lin on the movie, the fourth installment in the popular franchise The Fast and the Furious.

Like *The Fast and the Furious* and *2 Fast 2 Furious* before it, *Fast & Furious* stars Vin Diesel as Dominic Toretto and the late Paul Walker as Brian O'Conner. The character of Gisele, new to the film series, was well-suited for Gadot for a few reasons. One of the most important was Gadot's knowledge of weapons from her experience in the Israeli Defense Forces. This made her character believable to audiences. Gadot was signed to a three-movie deal, which allowed her character to evolve for audiences. Director Justin Lin explained in *Elle* magazine, "I still remember her audition tape. A lot of other actresses were playing the scene. But Gal made me feel like, I want to really get to know more about her. There was so much depth, like a life prior. There's an unknown about her."[6]

Lin eventually got to know Gadot during the audition process and realized she was just right for the part of Gisele. In an interview with an Israeli newspaper, Gadot stated that she felt one of the reasons director Justin Lin chose her for the role was because of her time in the Israeli military and her knowledge of weapons.

Gadot's experience in the military also made her capable of performing her own stunts in the movie, another bonus for the film franchise and its fans. Some of those stunts included riding a motorcycle, something Gadot has always loved. It has even been reported that the actress owns a 2006 Ducati Monster-S2R motorcycle. She said about practicing for the role in the film, "I was

Gadot's role in *Fast Five* allowed the actress to make use of her motorcycle-riding skills. It was her second movie in the Fast and Furious franchise.

able to practice with the most professional people on Earth and whatever I did I always felt very safe because I knew that they had my back, so it was easy and was cool."[7]

Since her roles in the Fast and the Furious movies, Gadot has given up riding motorcycles. In a July 2015 talk with *Interview* magazine, Gadot explained that she stopped riding motorcycles once she became a mother. She feels that the pastime is too risky for someone devoted to caring for her children.[8]

"Always in Our Hearts"

In all, Gadot appeared in three of the Fast and the Furious franchise films—stories four, five, and six in the franchise. After *Fast & Furious* and *Fast Five*, Gadot's character Gisele was killed in *Fast & Furious 6*. Because she didn't appear in the seventh film, she was not present with the other cast members when a tragedy occurred surrounding one of her castmates.

While on a break from filming *Furious 7*, the 2015 Fast and the Furious film, costar Paul Walker died in a car crash. His death on November 30, 2013, shocked fans of the series, which prominently features car stunts and stunt driving. Stars of the film series have continued to pay tribute to Walker over the years. On the second anniversary of his death, Gadot posted a photo of herself with Walker on her Instagram feed, stating "Always in our hearts."[9]

In a 2017 podcast with the *Hollywood Reporter's Awards Chatter*, Gadot stated that she had still not fully processed Paul Walker's tragic death. Because she saw

Gadot poses at a film festival in Marseille, France, with her *Fast Five* costars. The 2011 promotional photo shows Gadot posing with Elsa Pataky, Paul Walker, and Dwayne Johnson.

• •

Walker only periodically on film sets she felt that she could one day run into him again. "I wasn't in touch with him between projects," she explained. She went on to state that, "some part of me thinks that I'm going to see Paul, because that's just the way that it is for me." She described his death as "super, super tragic," and paid tribute to him at the time on her Facebook page. She stated in the *Awards Chatter* podcast, "I loved Paul and adored him from the very first moment that I met him because he was so grounded and down to Earth and the cutest, coolest dude—and so real as well."[10]

Other Fast and Furious stars have also paid tribute to Paul Walker throughout the years. On the fourth anniversary of Walker's death, the series star, Vin Diesel, praised his friend on Instagram. "No matter where you are, whether it's a quarter mile away or halfway across the world, you'll always be family."[11]

Family has been an important theme of the Fast and the Furious franchise, which focuses on the tight bond of the characters. In 2017, Gadot was asked to present the Generation Award to her former cast members during the MTV Movie & TV Awards. During that presentation, Gadot brought up the theme of family, referring not only to the bond of the characters, but also to the lasting bond between the cast members and the late Paul Walker. "Before I was Wonder Woman," she said onstage, "I got a call that would change my life. I was asked to be a part of the Fast and Furious franchise. The stunts may get bigger and crazier, but the heartbeat of the franchise, the reason people keep packing theaters over and over again is family. A diverse group of people who stick together, no matter what, through onscreen adventure and real-life tragedy."[12]

> "Family ... A diverse group of people who stick together, no matter what, through onscreen adventure and real-life tragedy."

After the Fast and the Furious

After her last Fast and the Furious film, *Fast & Furious 6,* Gadot gained more experience acting in different movies with different directors. The actress appeared in several

In *Keeping Up with the Joneses*, Gadot plays a spy along with her husband, played by Jon Hamm. The film was released in 2016, the same year Gadot was introduced as Wonder Woman in the DC Extended Universe.

films in supporting roles, including the 2016 action movies *Criminal* and *Triple 9.*

In *Triple 9,* which starred Chiwetel Ejiofor and Casey Affleck, Gadot plays the character of Elena Vlaslov, sister of the film's Russian crime boss villain, played by Kate Winslet. In *Criminal,* Gadot plays the supporting role of Jill Pope, wife of the main character, played by Kevin Costner.

While both *Criminal* and *Triple 9* are action films, Gadot did not get the chance to use her physical and weapons training. That opportunity actually occurred in Gadot's first role in a comedy, *Keeping Up with the Joneses.*

Roles That Could Have Been

The life of an actress means auditions for roles that sometimes go to other people. Gadot is no exception. In addition to the Bond Girl role that went to another actress, Gadot also auditioned for several other roles that did not go to her. Some were in the comic book universe that she later conquered. She auditioned for the role of Nebula in Marvel's 2014 *Guardians of the Galaxy,* a role that went to actress Karen Gillan. She was offered the role of Faora in 2013's *Man of Steel.* She could not play the villain from Superman's home planet of Krypton, however, because she was pregnant with her first child. The role instead went to actress Antje Traue. Of course, Gadot would meet up with the Superman universe a few years later in her first role as Wonder Woman in *Batman v. Superman: Dawn of Justice.*

In the 2016 film, Gadot played the part of Natalie Jones, a government spy who works undercover with her husband, played by actor Jon Hamm. The couple moves into a suburban neighborhood and is eventually found out by their neighbors, played by Isla Fisher and Zach Galifianakis.

The year 2016 brought Gadot to the movie world outside the Fast and the Furious franchise. In addition to *Criminal, Triple 9,* and *Keeping Up with the Joneses,* 2016 was also the year Gadot was introduced to the comic book film world as Wonder Woman in *Batman v. Superman: Dawn of Justice.*

Chapter Four

Wonder Woman

· ·

When Warner Brothers decided to look for an actress to play the part of Wonder Woman in its DC Extended Universe, the company knew it had to keep the project top secret. The plan was to introduce Wonder Woman in *Batman v. Superman: Dawn of Justice* to prepare fans for the upcoming feature length film *Wonder Woman*. There was a lot at stake with the multimillion-dollar project, so keeping details secret was important to the franchise. Even the actresses auditioning for the role did not know more than who the director was.

Warner Brothers had started its DC Extended Universe films in 2013 with the release of *Man of Steel*, starring Henry Cavill as Superman. When Gal Gadot went on her first audition for the role, she assumed it was for the role of Selina Kyle, who is the alter ego of supervillain Catwoman. Catwoman had been played

The second film in the DC Extended Universe, *Batman v. Superman: Dawn of Justice,* introduced Wonder Woman in a supporting role to fans. Ben Affleck plays Batman in the ongoing series.

on the big screen by several actresses, including Halle Berry, Anne Hathaway, and Michelle Pfeiffer.

It was not until Gadot returned for a second audition to read with actor Ben Affleck that she was told that she was auditioning for the role of Diana Prince, the character who would be Wonder Woman for the new Warner Brothers franchise.

When she got the role of the new superhero, Gadot was excited. She would have to enter a tough physical training plan, despite her already good physical shape and military training. She appeared for the first time to DC fans at the end of the *Batman v. Superman: Dawn of Justice* trailer, helping Batman and Superman unite against a larger-than-life villain.

The journey from the first audition to the introduction to the intense comic fan world was a long one. There was a tremendous amount to learn and achieve, but it was an endeavor that Gadot took very seriously.

An Amazonian Workout

According to msn.com, Gadot's training for the role of Wonder Woman led her to gain 17 pounds (7.7 kilograms) of muscle.[1] For her first role of the three films about the DC superheroes, she worked out in gyms alongside her male costars Ben Affleck, who plays Batman, and Henry Cavill, who plays Superman.

The most intense training, however, came for Gadot's own starring role as Amazonian horseback-riding princess Diana Prince in the second film in Gadot's contract with DC and Warner Brothers, *Wonder Woman*.

Gadot and *Justice League* director Zack Snyder play around on set. Physical training for the film took months, and Gadot worked out alongside her costars.

This role would require nearly superhuman skills to portray the iconic superhero.

She talked about her difficult training on the talk show *Live with Kelly and Ryan* in 2017. She even had to do the interview standing up, admitting that she had thrown out her back during a workout. Discussing her *Wonder Woman* training, she said,

> I was training for six months prior to the shoot. And six hours a day. I did two hours of gym work, two hours of fight choreography, and two hours of horseback riding. Which is super hard. When people used to tell me, "Yeah I do sports I ride horses," I was like, "That's not sport. The horse does everything." No! No! You'd be surprised — it's so painful.[2]

When asked if her training in the Israeli military helped her training to be a superhero, Gadot explained that the preparation for the film was much more intensive than the military training.[3]

Probably the most impressive part of Gadot's workout and training for the film happened after it was over. As a common practice in filmmaking, some scenes must be refilmed after the production is over. Reshoots may be necessary for a number of reasons, and Gadot had to do some scene reshoots for *Wonder Woman* when she was five months pregnant with her second child. The physically demanding role continued with Gadot's preparation for her performance in *Justice League,* the third film in her three-film contract with Warner Brothers.

The introduction of Wonder Woman to audiences was a success. Audiences saw Gadot in *Batman v.*

Patty Jenkins: A Director's View

Wonder Woman director Patty Jenkins was born in Victorville, California, in 1971. Her father was a captain in the US Air Force but died during a training exercise when Patty was seven. She and her mother and sister settled in Lawrence, Kansas. Jenkins told the *Hollywood Reporter* that growing up around the military helped her learn the skills needed to be a director. She said, "You need to be reliable, on time, confident, calm, all of those things you see demonstrated in the military."[4]

As a college student, Jenkins studied painting at New York City's Cooper Union. That's where she took a film course that helped spark her career. After graduating in 1993, she worked on music videos and commercials before moving to Los Angeles to try her hand at directing. Her first feature length film was *Monster*, a 2003 film about real-life serial killer Aileen Wuornos. Actress Charlize Theron won several awards for the film, including the Academy Award and Golden Globe for Best Actress. Before *Wonder Woman,* Jenkins also directed episodes of television shows such as *Entourage* and *Arrested Development*. Her direction of the 2011 pilot of the show *The Killing* won her a nomination for an Emmy Award.

Gadot takes direction from *Wonder Woman* director Patty Jenkins on the set. The women collaborated on the best way to present the character on film.

Superman: Dawn of Justice and eagerly anticipated her role in *Wonder Woman*. Instead of being directed by Zack Snyder, however, the film about the female superhero would be directed by a woman—Patty Jenkins.

When Jenkins began directing *Wonder Woman*, she kept with the physical training that the DC characters needed to look in shape on film. Diana Prince is from an island of Amazonian warrior women who are physically larger and stronger than humans. To make this point come across on film, Jenkins hired athletes instead of models to play the parts of the women. She sent all of them to six months of boot camp.[5]

Working with Director Patty Jenkins

When Gal Gadot was hired to be Wonder Woman, she was working with Zack Snyder. *Batman v. Superman: Dawn of Justice* was the first film appearance for the superhero, and the director of *Wonder Woman* had not even been hired yet. Would the director of *Wonder Woman* work well with Gadot, who had already been signed on for two more films? According to *Time* magazine, when Patty Jenkins was hired

> "Gal is the perfect Wonder Woman from many aspects."
>
> —*Wonder Woman* director Patty Jenkins

as the director, she was concerned about having to work with an actress who was hired by another film crew for another project entirely. But after working with Gadot,

Jenkins considered herself very fortunate to have such a good person to work with her on the project.

Patty Jenkins discussed in an article from ynetnews. com, "Gal is the perfect Wonder Woman from many aspects. I believe that the spirit of the actor you choose for the film is the most important overall. If the actor fails to understand the spirit of the project, it won't work."[6]

Jenkins felt that Gadot's personality was not far off from Diana Prince's personality:

> We needed someone who could play the role of Wonder Woman on the big screen, but we got someone who plays the role on and off-screen. We got someone whose instincts are similar to those of the character she plays. She really is courteous and enduring, but she's no sucker. She isn't gentle and fragile. She understands very well what is going on around her, and she's funny and pleasant as well. She calmed me down many times and knew how to deal with me when I arrived on the set nervous.[7]

Gadot had equally positive things to say about working with Jenkins:

> All my life I've been working with male directors which I've really enjoyed. And I'm lucky in that I've worked with men who have a lot of respect for women. But working with a woman is a different experience. It feels like the communication is different. We talk about emotions. With Patty, it's a thing now, we communicate with our eyes. She doesn't need to say a thing. If I'm hurt, she feels the pain. It's a whole different connection that I have with her. She's also brilliant, she's bright, she's fierce, she's sharp. She knows exactly what she wants *Wonder Woman* to be.[8]

A Strong Character

Although the character of Diana Prince was created in 1941, she had not been portrayed as a major film character on the big screen before. The filmmakers had to think a lot about how to portray the character to audiences. Before that point, women had only played supporting roles as superheroes. DC superheroes include Starfire and Raven from Teen Titans, Harley Quinn from Suicide Squad, and Supergirl, Batwoman, and Catwoman. All of these characters played supporting roles or worked in a group without their own storylines or the origin stories that male superheroes seemed to have. Developing Wonder Woman for the big screen was an important opportunity to send a positive message to women and girls, not to mention to boys and men. Gadot worked with Jenkins, a longtime Wonder Woman fan, to develop a character with the right message.

"For a long time, people didn't know how to approach the story," Gadot said in an interview about her collaboration with Jenkins. "When Patty and I had our creative conversations about the character, we realized that Diana can still be a normal woman, one with very high values, but still a woman. She can be sensitive. She is smart and independent and emotional. She can be confused. She can lose her confidence. She can have confidence. She is everything. She has a human heart."[9]

In the film, Gadot's character, Diana Prince, is raised on the island of Themyscira, an island of only Amazonian warrior women, magically hidden from the view of the rest of the world. The warriors were created by the god Zeus to protect humankind. Diana

Lynda Carter: Wonder Woman on the Small Screen

Gal Gadot is not the only actress to have played Wonder Woman onscreen. From 1975 to 1979, actress Lynda Carter played Wonder Woman in a popular television series. Born in Phoenix, Arizona, in 1951, Carter studied classical dance and drama. Carter entered beauty pageants, and—similar to the way Gadot won the Miss Israel pageant—became Miss USA in 1973. After that she began to study acting.

When Carter first got the role of Wonder Woman, there were very few shows on television with a female lead. She told British newspaper *Daily Mail,* "TV executives didn't think there was a market for a female holding a show like *Wonder Woman.* Women were buying all their products, yet men dominated the shows."[10]

She explained to *Variety* magazine in 2016 that Wonder Woman is an important icon for women. "We're still fighting the same fight. We still need more female role models." She said, "Wonder Woman is much more than a cartoon character. She's fighting for truth and justice and the secret self that exists in all women and girls. There's a moral fiber and a goodness about her that all women have."[11]

grows up not realizing her history and true identity as an important part in the protection of humanity. She enters the human world with World War I soldier Steve Trevor, played by actor Chris Pine. Diana believes the villain Ares, the Greek god of war, is responsible for the destruction of the world, and she leaves the protected island to go stop the war.

The details of the film's plot are not as important as its overall message of peace. As Gadot told *Variety* magazine, "We cared a lot about simplifying Wonder Woman's agenda, because it is simple. It was her heart that we cared about, not her being this warrior." She explained, "For her it was very important to not just portray her as a goddess, but to tell a very simple story of someone who believes in good and believes that people should be happy and lead safe, happy lives."[12]

Both Gadot and Jenkins felt it was important that the work that the character of Diana Prince does in the human world be done with that positive message of peace they set out to deliver. The character has always been known as a feminist hero and a "warrior of peace." Besides her shield and wrist guards for protection, Wonder Woman's main weapon is her "lasso of truth." When the golden rope is tied around someone, he or she can't help but tell the truth. The weapon itself provides a positive message, so Gadot and Jenkins wanted the character to live up to that positive message as well.

Moviegoers seemed to agree with the positive message and supported the film as the latest addition to the DC Extended Universe. The film earned $841.74 million worldwide in 2017. That figure makes the film

Gadot worked closely with the film's costume designers to make sure Wonder Woman's costume, shown here on display at the 2016 Licensing Expo in Las Vegas, Nevada, would allow her to perform in comfort.

one of the highest-grossing superhero origin movies of all time, according to *Forbes* magazine.[13]

Looking Like a Superhero

Looking like Wonder Woman meant more than just working out. The costume was also an important part of being a hero. Gadot admitted that when she first put on the costume designed for her to wear in the films, she could not believe how tight it was. She joked that she couldn't breathe in it. She admits going back and forth with the costume department about the outfit before finally getting it right. "I made it very clear that I needed to have some oxygen going through my body to shoot the movie. We adjusted the costume and I wore it every single day, and we shot over 117 days. The new version was great. I can even sleep in it. It's like pyjamas."[14]

Gadot told *Variety* magazine about the costume:

It takes me five minutes to take it off and 20 minutes to put the entire costume on. I've spent a year in it, from *Batman v Superman* to *Justice League* to [*Wonder Woman*]. From one movie to the next, it got more and more comfortable. I love the way it looks, but it didn't feel comfortable at the beginning. I feel better in it now, which was super important because the role is so physical.[15]

One of the main things that filmmakers wanted to do to keep the message positive was to keep with the traditional superhero look of Wonder Woman. Everything from the bodice, skirt, headband, wristbands, and lasso looks very similar to the ones in the original comic.

However, some fans missed the point. They judged Gadot's body—just the kind of criticism against women that Wonder Woman was trying to dispel by being a positive role model. "They said that I was too skinny and my boobs were too small," said Gadot. "They said my head was too big and my body was like a broomstick. I can take anything. It's just empty talk. I can understand that part of what I'm doing means being exposed. And part of being exposed is being under fire."[16]

CHAPTER FIVE

A Superhero Influence

The release of *Wonder Woman* in June of 2017 meant more than just a boost to Gal Gadot's career. It also meant a boost to the image of the feminist hero introduced for the first time in 1941. According to *Variety* magazine, the film opened with $103.1 million in ticket sales in the United States. With the worldwide release, the film had a $223 million opening around the globe.[1] The sales were much better than anticipated. And ticket sales only picked up pace after the opening weekend. Within six weeks of its release, the film had earned about $880 million, according to *Forbes* magazine. By the end of its theatrical release, it had earned the most of any superhero origin movie of all time.

Wonder Woman immediately generated a strong fan base. Audiences felt the movie showed the popular character with the strength of a superhero but the understanding and humanity they had wanted to see in other superheroes.

Even talk show host Oprah Winfrey became a devoted fan of the film. In June 2017 she declared a "Wonder Woman Day" to honor the film and its importance to young girls. To celebrate, she invited twenty-eight ten-year-old girls to her home in Los Angeles, California, to celebrate the film. Winfrey has always taken mentorship of young girls seriously, as the founder of the Oprah Winfrey Leadership Academy for Girls. As with many of the projects that Winfrey promotes, her support of *Wonder Woman* and its positive feminist message exposed many people in her viewing audience to the film.

Thanks to high expectations and word of mouth, word spread quickly about the new film starring a strong female lead. After the release of the film, *Wonder Woman* producers sent director Patty Jenkins a social media listing of things a kindergarten teacher noticed her students do and say in class within just one week of the movie's release. The teacher posted her list on Twitter, and it spread to many readers. The list the teacher tweeted read, "On Monday, a boy who was obsessed with Iron Man told me he had asked his parents for a new Wonder Woman lunchbox." Another read, "A little girl said 'When I grow up I want to speak hundreds of languages like Diana.'" Still another girl asked her parents to "revamp her Beauty and the Beast birthday party in THREE DAYS because she simply had to have a Wonder Woman party." And to recognize the film's theme of working together for a common good, there was another important observation the teacher made. It read, "Seven girls playing together during recess on Tuesday, saying that since they all wanted to be Wonder

Lunchboxes and other merchandise bearing Wonder Woman's likeness became popular again thanks to Gadot's portrayal.

• • • • • • • • • • • • • • • • • • • •

Woman they had agreed to be Amazons and not fight but work together to defeat evil."[2]

The social media message from the kindergarten teacher ended with a final message. It said, "Consider this your friendly reminder that if this movie completely changed the way these girls and boys thought about themselves and the world in a week, imagine what the next generation will achieve if we give them more movies like Wonder Woman." Gal Gadot retweeted the message and wrote her own reply. It said, "Wow the last paragraph really gave me the chills. So true. So powerful. Gives me a huge drive to dive in and work on the next one."[3]

From the Director's Chair

Getting the character right was important to the film's director, Patty Jenkins. She has admitted to being a fan of the original Wonder Woman comics and the 1970s television series starring Lynda Carter. She felt bringing Wonder Woman to the movie screen for the first time was important. She wanted the character to have those qualities that she admired when she read the comics and watched the TV show as a child. "I followed the rules that I can believe in," she told *Glamour* magazine. "Wonder Woman doesn't hurt people for fun. She doesn't use violence unless she has to, and when she has to, she's incredibly adept."[4]

Jenkins explained that one of the unique things about creating the Wonder Woman character for the big screen was her view of the world, coming from an island of only women. She explained to *Glamour* magazine that Diana Prince is "oblivious to sexism because she's never encountered it. So the greatest thing is that you're able to inadvertently comment on it all: She becomes aware of sexism as she's observing it, and through her eyes, we see how absurd it is."[5]

Jenkins also felt that Wonder Woman should stand out among the other superhero films in the DC Extended Universe by not being as dark as some of the other origin stories in the franchise, such as those of Batman

Actress Lynda Carter starred as Wonder Woman in the 1970s television series of the same name. Carter did not appear in the first Wonder Woman movie with Gadot, but she may appear in the second film.

or Superman. In an interview with News Corp Australia that was printed in the *Herald Sun,* Jenkins claims, "For Wonder Woman to be dark would have been a huge shame. It wouldn't be right. I am happy she brings a bit of lightheartedness to the DC Universe."[6]

Jenkins appeared with the cast for an interview on *Good Morning America* shortly after the movie was released. She explained that the character represented more than just female empowerment, but that Wonder Woman represented the journey of any person who wants to feel like a hero in their own life. She explained,

> I'm a huge believer in the story of becoming a hero and the myth of superhero movies. I always have believed in it. So the idea of getting to share something with kids of the world and adults of the world of all kinds … The story of someone who wants to be a hero and take a journey to becoming a real hero and [learn] what that is, is something beautiful. So I hope they have a great time, and I hope they love it, and I hope they laugh, but I also hope they feel inspired to be a hero in their own life and learn love and thoughtfulness as well as strength.[7]

Message Received

Gal Gadot understood the impact that the character of Diana Prince was having on people. She told *Entertainment Weekly,* "I feel that I've got the opportunity to set a great role model for girls to look up to a strong, active, compassionate, loving, positive woman and I think it's so important. It's about time that somebody will do that and I'm very privileged and honored to be the one."[8]

Gadot explained in an interview with *Variety* magazine what she thought people saw in the on-screen character that inspired them. "She's relatable. She has the heart of a human and is very compassionate, but her experiences—or lack of them, her naiveté, really—make her interested in everything around her and able to view

More Heroes to Come

With the release and success of *Wonder Woman,* film companies have decided to continue with more heroines on the big screen. The Marvel Universe is cashing in on the female superhero genre with Captain Marvel. Actress Brie Larson will be playing the superhero in the film. This will not only create an additional big screen hero for Marvel, but it will also provide competition for the DC Extended Universe. Larson's character, Carol Danvers, is a major in the air force, and the superhero role required some intense physical training. Larson felt a similar responsibility that Gadot felt when portraying the superhero. She was apprehensive at first to take on such a big responsibility of playing a strong, heroic role model. "Ultimately, I couldn't deny the fact that this movie is everything I care about, everything that's progressive and important and meaningful, and a symbol I wished I would've had growing up. I really, really feel like it's worth it if it can bring understanding and confidence to young women—I'll do it."[9]

the world in a way that we'd all like to: with a genuine curiosity."[10]

In her interview with *Entertainment Weekly* about a month after the film's release, she was asked if she thought the undertaking felt like a big responsibility. She replied, "It is a big responsibility. We knew we wanted to tell a story that would inspire people: women, men, boys, and girls. And we didn't want to just show a generic story of a superhero coming of age. We wanted her to be full and whole. This is the first time we are telling this story and I feel like for so many boys, they have great role models to work with. They have Superman and Batman and Spiderman and the list goes on and on. And they are strong and almighty and they are positive and active and proactive."[11]

> "It is a big responsibility. We knew we wanted to tell a story that would inspire people: women, men, boys, and girls."

Gadot was able to see what an influence she had on people when she attended the 2017 Comic-Con in San Diego, California. During these comic conventions, fans gather to hear people speak about film and comic projects. The conventions also have panel discussions with actors, directors, or producers who worked on some of the films. Fans have the opportunity to get autographs from the actors who played their favorite DC Extended Universe or Marvel film characters, among others.

To get the autographs at conventions, fans of all ages line up in front of tables that actors or directors sit behind to greet the public. At the San Diego Comic-Con in 2017, many young girls dressed up like Wonder Woman to get Gadot's autograph. One girl was caught on video as she was crying with tears of joy as she met her idol. *Variety* magazine tweeted a video of the interaction, and thousands of people began talking about it online. Online news outlets reposted the video as well. In the video, Gadot can be seen holding the crying girl's hand and comforting her as she gave her an autograph and listened to her talk. The video demonstrated both the

At the 2017 Comic-Con International, Gadot met young fans and signed autographs. She appeared alongside her *Justice League* costars, including Jason Momoa (*right*).

impact that Wonder Woman can have on young girls and the sensitivity and seriousness with which Gadot takes the responsibility of playing the classic heroine on screen.

In a November 2017, interview on *Today* with Willie Geist, Gadot explained that she liked the way Diana Prince was portrayed because the character had more depth and reality than most female heroes seen in movies. She stated that when you normally see a strong woman in a movie, it means that "she's tough, she's distant, she's cold." Gadot knew the Wonder Woman character should be more than that. She asked, "How do you tell a story about a woman that is super strong and make everyone feel like they can relate to her story?... We showed it in the movie—that you can be vulnerable and you can be innocent in a way, and truthful and loving, like you can have it all."[12]

Jenkins explained in an interview that there are great signs that *Wonder Woman* has reached more than just an audience of young girls looking for a strong female role model. The director said that her own son's reaction to the film said a lot about what she was trying to accomplish. "My son doesn't care about what I do that much," she said. "But he plays with superheroes and he cares about those things." She said that watching him express a desire for a Wonder Woman action figure was rewarding because it meant that she was a serious character to him. She stated, "It's been amazing to watch this character come back to that generation in such an authentic way and everything she stands for, right alongside all these other great characters."[13]

The Original Heroine

Like many superhero comics, Wonder Woman was first published during World War II. The idea of searching for truth and justice appealed to many Americans.

The role women played on the home front during World War II also helped make the character appealing at the time. According to the National World War II Museum, nearly 350,000 American women volunteered for the Women's Army Corps, the women's branch of the US Army.[14] While women at the time did not have combat roles like men did, many nurses worked near

The Lasso of Truth

One of the things that makes Wonder Woman a different hero than many of the others in the classic comic book world is her method of fighting. Instead of having a weapon that can strike or injure her enemies, Wonder Woman's weapon is a "lasso of truth." When wrapped around someone, the lasso magically causes the person to tell the truth. This makes the heroine's message more about justice than about defeating a particular enemy. The lasso of truth was always part of Wonder Woman's character, even from the start of the comic back in 1941. The comic's creator was a psychologist named William Moulton Marston. He was also an inventor who worked on an early version of the lie detector.[15] Adapting the concept of lie detection as a superhero power is one of the reasons Marston's initial Wonder Woman comic appealed to audiences.

Wonder Woman's lasso of truth is her most valuable weapon. The lasso forces anyone who is surrounded by it to tell the truth. The lasso of truth was established in the original Wonder Woman comics.

the front lines of the war and were in danger just as the men were. The Women's Army Corps was formed by the government during the war and was made up of women from different branches of the armed forces. Many of these women worked in offices. Others served as nurses or did assembly or repair work on airplanes. Some drove trucks or worked in laboratories.

Women who did not serve in the military during the war may have worked in factories in the United States, keeping the US economy moving and supplying goods for the military and the war effort. Many of the factory jobs supplied the military with the weapons and vehicles it needed to fight.

One of the most popular recruiting campaigns for women during the war featured a picture of a factory worker called a riveter, whose job it was to drill short metal bolts, called rivets, into planes and ships to hold plates of metal together. The determined-looking character in the poster became known as Rosie the Riveter, with her hair pulled back and sleeves rolled up, showing her arm flexed with a tight fist. A voice bubble above her head said "We Can Do It!" The image helped echo the sentiments of many women during the time. They felt empowered to do their part to help the war effort.

Starting a comic book with a female superhero in the same year the United States entered World War II was good timing for DC Comics. The comic was well received, and readers identified with Diana Prince, just as they identified with Rosie the Riveter. The comic was set during the war, and the original story depicted Diana leaving the island of Amazon women with Steve Trevor to fight in World War II. The villain in the comics was female as well. Baroness von Gunther was a Nazi,[16] similar to the enemies and villains that Americans read about every day when they read about the war. Many scenes in the original comics depict Wonder Woman fighting Nazis. Even the Wonder Woman television show of the 1970s, starring Lynda Carter as Wonder woman, was set during World War II.

In contrast to the original comic, the 2017 film *Wonder Woman* was set during World War I instead of during World War II. However, many of the concepts of fighting evil during a world war are the same.

The character of Wonder Woman has gone through many changes throughout her seventy-five-year history. At first she was criticized for being inappropriate for young readers, largely due to her attire. She was stripped of her superpowers during the 1960s. At one point, she even gave up her role as a hero entirely so she could marry Steve Trevor. Long-time readers saw the changes in the character and how they reflected the way feminism was seen during different time periods.

In 1972, the feminist magazine *Ms.,* which was cofounded by feminist and political activist Gloria Steinem, featured Wonder Woman on the cover of its first issue. Steinem saw at the time that the character and the changes that she went through over the decades could help start a discussion about feminism. According to *Slate* magazine, Steinem had explained at the time, "Wonder Woman symbolizes many of the values of the women's culture that feminists are now trying to introduce into the mainstream: strength and self-reliance for women; sisterhood and mutual support among women; peacefulness and esteem for human life; a diminishment both of 'masculine' aggression and of the belief that violence is the only way of solving conflicts."[17]

CHAPTER SIX

The Justice League's Best Gal

· ·

Gal Gadot's role as Wonder Woman means more than just a single summer blockbuster for Warner Brothers Entertainment Inc. Her position in the DC Extended Universe means much more for the legacy of the franchise. The success of the Wonder Woman film helped the franchise know what audiences liked and what to pursue for future films.

With the reboot of the film version of Batman, played by Ben Affleck, and Superman, played by Henry Cavill, the DC Extended Universe was off to a good start. Adding successful new characters was necessary in order for the films to continue making money andto keep fans wanting to see more. Gal Gadot played a part in helping the franchise continue its success.

But it is always a gamble when a new project begins. Hollywood stars often get millions of dollars to act in a single film. The more popular the star and the more successful the franchise, the more money the actor can get. For example, Robert Downey Jr., who plays Iron Man in the Marvel Cinematic Universe, went from receiving a relatively low salary for his first Iron Man film to being one of the highest paid actors in Hollywood, according to *Forbes* magazine.

Similar increases in salary take place among actors working on films in the Marvel Cinematic Universe. One example is Chris Hemsworth, who plays Thor. Hemsworth was relatively unknown when he was first cast as Thor, and he reportedly received $200,000 to act

Gadot appeared in *Justice League*, the third film in the DC Extended Universe, along with (l-r) Ezra Miller as the Flash, Henry Cavill as Superman, Ray Fisher as Cyborg, Ben Affleck as Batman, and Jason Momoa as Aquaman.

in his first Thor film. But after a few films in his role as one of the Avengers, he reportedly earned more than $5 million in *Avengers: Age of Ultron*.

Gal Gadot was in a similar situation when she was signed on by Warner Brothers to play Wonder Woman. She was to receive $300,000 for each of the three films that were part of her contract: *Batman v. Superman: Dawn of Justice, Wonder Woman,* and *Justice League.* At the time, although she was in the Fast and the Furious films, she was not a main character and had not handled a starring role before. Just as her *Justice League* costars had done, she had to show that she could attract audiences and help the franchise succeed. And she did prove herself, within just months of her first starring role.

As *Justice League* was released in November of 2017, Gadot found herself in a good position to rise to the top of the Hollywood ladder, based on her influences and positive message. At that point, she had not yet negotiated a contract to work on *Wonder Woman 2* but was securely in the position to make any improvement she wished.

Filming *Justice League*

Justice League was directed by Zack Snyder, the same director as *Batman v Superman: Dawn of Justice.* In addition to Ben Affleck as Batman and Henry Cavill as Superman, the film starred Gal Gadot as Wonder Woman, Ezra Miller as the Flash, Jason Momoa as Aquaman, and Ray Fisher as Cyborg. As with the other DC Extended Universe films, the actors went through rigorous physical training for their roles. According to

Wonder Woman of the Year

To coincide with the November 2017 release of *Justice League*, *GQ* magazine chose Gal Gadot as their "Wonder Woman of the Year." The men's fashion and fitness magazine's twenty-second annual Men of the Year issue featured three men and one woman—Gal Gadot—for its 2017 influential picks. The other honorees included late-night talk show host Stephen Colbert, football player and activist Colin Kaepernick, and basketball star Kevin Durant. The magazine did a photo shoot with each of the influential people to feature on each of its four different magazine covers.

Men's Health magazine, each star worked with a trainer on a different routine for getting into shape. Jason Momoa prepared to play Aquaman by doing a lot of rock-wall climbing and pull-ups. Henry Cavill, Ben Affleck, and Ezra Miller added strength and mass to their bodies by doing heavy weight lifting. Gadot gained muscle weight along with her other costars by using stationary bikes and rowing machines. She also did squats and pull-ups to add to her strength.

Similar to her work on the Fast and the Furious films, Gadot worked with a close ensemble cast for *Justice League*. One of the film's producers, Chuck Roven, told *People* magazine that the "chemistry between the cast was better than we could have imagined." He explained that the cast connected both on the set and off the set as well. "Usually, in between setups a cast will migrate and go back to their trailers," he said of other productions. "But for most of the shoot, not only in between takes but in between setups, the cast would hang with each other. Whenever I would turn around or arrive on set there they would be, telling each other a story, an anecdote, or laughing."[1]

In a November 19, 2017, interview on *Today* with Willie Geist, Gadot talked about working on *Justice League* and being part of an ensemble cast. "It was great for me, because after six months of shooting *Wonder Woman*, I got the opportunity to share the stage with more talented, wonderful people, and it was not all on my shoulders, and it was a lot of fun."[2]

By the time *Justice League* was released, the film *Wonder Woman* had already been out for about five months. The character was still fresh in people's minds. Fans were excited to be getting the chance to see the character again in another film so soon after *Wonder Woman*. In a November 15 appearance on *Live with Kelly and Ryan* to promote *Justice League*, Gadot was asked by host Ryan Seacrest about the impact the role of Wonder Woman has had. "There are so many fans of all ages," he said. "What do they say to you?"

She replied, "The feedback is really, really amazing, and I'm still taking it all in and overwhelmed by it. It's super positive, and I'm the link to the character, you know? It's not *me*, it's Wonder Woman. So it's amazing and it's incredible to see how much of an impact this character has on people."[3]

In response, host Kelly Ripa helped clarify Gadot's sentiments by discussing the popularity of Wonder

Woman Halloween costumes that year. Having worn one herself, Ripa stated that the costume—especially the metal bracelets for deflecting bullets—allows ordinary people to experience what it might be like to feel like

> **"It's amazing and it's incredible to see how much of an impact this character has on people."**

a superhero. The hosts displayed a comical photograph of their crew members, both male and female, dressed in Wonder Woman costumes for their Halloween episode just weeks earlier.

Gadot's Wonder Woman has influenced a new generation of young girls craving a superhero they can identify with.

The rejuvinated popularity of Wonder Woman after the film's release was a positive step for the character. Only a year earlier, the United Nations (UN), an international organization dedicated to world peace, had named the fictional superhero as an honorary ambassador. However, the UN, formed after the end of World War II, dropped the ambassadorship when it received a petition signed by more than 44,000 people. Their complaint? They felt that a character wearing such a skimpy outfit should not be honored as a positive role model. The overwhelming response that both boys and girls have had to Wonder Woman shows that the character does in fact have serve as a positive role model.

Facing Challenges

For Gadot, there was no break between shooting *Wonder Woman* and *Justice League*. During the last three months of the shoot, Gadot was pregnant with her second child. She described in an interview on *Live with Kelly and Ryan* that she felt very ill during that time from morning sickness, which is common during the first three months of pregnancy. She explained that she was particularly bothered by the bright lights on the set that were needed for the special effects scenes. She wore sunglasses to help block the light, but she explained that her assistant tried to help keep her secret. Her assistant would stay near her with a bucket in case of emergencies when she felt ill. She claimed that her assistant would even help by making loud noises to muffle the sound of Gadot vomiting.

The audience laughed as Gadot told her story to Kelly Ripa and Ryan Seacrest. "I didn't say anything to

Gadot appeared at the 74th Annual Golden Globe Awards while she was expecting her second child. This pregnancy coincided with her portrayal of Wonder Woman during the *Justice League* shoot.

anyone," she explained. "And I thought no one knew, but everyone knew apparently."[4] Even though going to work while feeling sick and working on such a physically demanding role was difficult, it was still very early in her pregnancy and not apparent to film viewers.

In an interview with the *Mirror* online, Gadot explained that in the end, she didn't mind working on *Justice League* and doing some *Wonder Woman* reshoots while pregnant. "It didn't hinder the process," she said. "I could still do the action stuff and the physical scenes. And now, it's nice to look at the movie and know that Maya is in the movie with me in some way. I love that."[5]

The *Justice League* film did not do as well financially as *Wonder Woman*. In fact, it was the lowest-earning film of the DC Extended Universe, earning $222 million in the United States and just over $646 million worldwide.[6] Although the numbers may seem high, they are far short of the projected goals set by producers and investors.

The film also met with trouble before it was even finished. Director Zack Snyder had a family tragedy, which caused him and his wife, Deborah, who was a producer on the film, to leave the production early. The couple's twenty-year old daughter, Autumn, tragically committed suicide. The couple knew they needed to attend to family matters instead of continuing with the film.

The project was taken over by writer and director Joss Whedon, who was credited as one of the film's screenwriters. Whedon was experienced with working on other superhero films. Among other projects, he was the writer and director of Marvel's *The Avengers* and *Avengers: Age of Ultron*.

Whedon's participation in the film had started even before Snyder left the film. He had been writing new material and doing some photography work on the project. When Snyder left the project, Whedon did extensive rewriting and reshoots, and then spent a lot of time on post-production, working to achieve a final result he knew would please Snyder. People involved with the film supported Snyder and the decision to hand the film over to Whedon. Gadot told *Empire Magazine* in an interview, "This is Zack Snyder's movie. Joss only did a few weeks of reshoots. He was Zack's guy and knew exactly what he [Zack] wanted to get."[7]

The Golden and Silver Ages of Comics

Wonder Woman and the entire Justice League got their start thanks to the popularity of comic books during the

A Team Event

Gal Gadot joined the cast of *Justice League* at a comic convention in Long Island, New York, in December 2017. The three-day Comic-Con ended with a panel discussion with the film's stars. Gadot thanked the fans and explained that they are the reason she and her castmates continue making the films. Ray Fisher, who plays Cyborg, spoke about the Justice League characters and what makes them resonate so strongly with audiences: "Each one has their specific trauma. What makes them special is the way they take that trauma and turn it into something positive."[8]

The original Wonder Woman comics were created by Harvard psychologist Dr. William Moulton Marston. The film *Professor Marston and the Wonder Women*, starring Luke Evans, describes the early history of the comic book.

• •

late 1930s through the mid-1950s. This era is considered by popular culture and art experts as the Golden Age of Comics. DC Comics, the leader in the industry, got its start under the name National Allied Publishing, run by a writer named Major Malcolm Wheeler-Nicholson. It was the first company to publish original comics on a regular basis, instead of just the short comic strips that appeared in newspapers. When the company was sold to Harry Donenfeld and Jack Liebowitz, it became known as DC, named after one of its popular series, *Detective Comics*. The company really took off in 1938 with the first issue of the Superman comic, created by Jerry Siegel and Joe Shuster. This first issue, simply called *Action Comics #1,* is now the world's most expense and valuable comic book collectors item. An issue in excellent condition sold for over $3 million in on online auction on eBay in 2014.[9]

Soon after the Golden Age of Comics came the next era of comic books. Sometimes known as the Silver Age, it was a time when superheroes who had their own followings and fan readerships would combine to form superhero alliances. This is when the Justice League comics began. The first issue was released in 1960, and the alliance brought together Superman, Batman, Wonder Woman, Aquaman, Flash, and Green Lantern.

In addition to the Justice League, DC came out with the Teen Titans during the 1960s, and Marvel followed suit with its own superhero teams. The Fantastic Four and Guardians of the Galaxy formed some of its most popular comic book properties. These teams continued to be popular through the decades that followed, with television cartoons and reboots, or reinventions, of origin stories of some of the characters.

CHAPTER SEVEN

Importance of Family

· · · · · · · · · · · ·

In addition to taking the role of Wonder Woman on the big screen seriously, Gal Gadot is also very serious about her own personal life and family. Gadot has been married since 2008, and the couple has two young daughters. Gadot gave birth to first daughter, Alma, in 2011. Daughter Maya was born in 2017. Gadot's husband has seen her acting career take off and has since become a successful businessman in his own right.

Family Life

Gadot explained in a March 2016 interview with *Glamour* magazine that she met her husband, Yaron Versano, a decade earlier through mutual friends at a party in Israel. "He's 10 years older than me," she said about the native Israeli. "He told me on our second date he was serious and wasn't going to wait more than two years to ask me to marry him. Fast-forward two years; he proposed. We were married in 2008."[1]

Gadot married Yaron Versano in 2008. The actress credits her husband's support for her success as an actress, wife, and mother.

In the interview, Gadot credits Versano and their relationship with her ability to be successful while having a family. She said, "Both of us said, 'No games. Let's just be honest and keep it simple.' I wouldn't be able to do what I do without him."[2]

Gadot also helped Versano's career get off the ground. In response to traveling so much for her work, Gadot and Versano were inspired by the possibility of a hotel business. Versano and his brother, Guy, are real estate developers, and some of their most valuable properties are hotels.

In a June 2017 article in *International Business Times,* Gadot explained how her career influenced the idea. "After I shot *Fast Four,*" she explained about her first film role in the United States for *Fast & Furious,* "My husband Yaron and I started traveling back and forth from Israel and the US, which was hard. We found ourselves staying in hotels all the time. We wanted to feel at home, which is when we discovered these apartments within a hotel in Los Angeles. It became the inspiration for Yaron's hotel, The Versano." The Versano is a hotel property in Tel Aviv, Israel. She went on to explain, "I think that Yaron and I make a really good team. I understand his career and he understands mine. We help each other progress in all areas of life. We're both very career driven."[3]

The hotel was owned by the family. Gadot used to help run the place with her husband and even helped do housekeeping tasks. They eventually sold the hotel in 2015 to Russian billionaire businessman Roman Abramovich for $26 million.[4]

Gadot understands that her husband is proud of her accomplishments. She explained in an interview with *Mirror* what has changed since she took on her Wonder Woman role and what has stayed the same. "He's my biggest fan," she said. "The only thing that changed is he has started training more because I became so strong!"[5]

Versano regularly shows off his wife on social media as well. He shows pictures of his wife at important events such as movie openings or awards ceremonies. He jokes about being married to the superhero, too. One Instagram post shows the couple together, with Versano wearing a T-shirt depicting two female figures. One is a traditional icon to symbolize a female wearing a dress, with the label "Your Wife" under it. The other shows an obvious outline of Wonder Woman with the label "My Wife" under it. Versano and Gadot are playfully pointing at each other in the photo. The picture went viral on social media. He added the hashtags #mywife and #therealwonderwoman.

A Social Family

Gadot's whole family is social on social media. Not only do Gadot and her husband, Yaron, use Instagram to keep fans updated about Gadot's accomplishments, but her mother does, too. Gadot's mother, Irit Gadot, posts Instagrams of her daughter at behind-the-scenes Hollywood events. The shots include posts of her daughter with costars Chris Pine and Ben Affleck and movie directors Patty Jenkins and Zack Snyder.

Gadot was just as complimentary to her husband. On Father's Day 2017, shortly after Versano's post, Gadot posted her own Instagram honor to her spouse. She posted a photo of frosted donuts with the words "Best Dad Ever" written on them. The message on the Instagram read: "To my other half, father of my children and love of my life @jaronvarsano. You are simply the best dad EVER! I couldn't ask for a better person to be the role model for my babies. You are our anchor, our hero and our heart. Love you to the moon and back. Happy Father's Day to all amazing dads out there. And to my own loving, protecting and amazing dad Michael. Celebrate all the great fathers and men in your life."[6]

Managing Family Life

Being a popular Hollywood actress while raising children is not as glamorous as people might think. In an interview with *Today* Show's Willie Geist, Gadot admitted that while *Wonder Woman* was being released in theaters and promoted on television she was at home with her children, caring for her newborn daughter. She said that she does laundry and cooks for her children, just like other mothers, and does not think of herself as a Hollywood icon. Instead, she expressed the difficulties of trying to juggle the jobs of raising children, maintaining her relationship with her husband, and dealing with the press to promote the film, all while thinking about the future of her career.

Learning to juggle family and career is something Gadot has had to work on over time. She told *Glamour* magazine in a March 2016 interview that she used to get

Even while raising her two daughters, Gadot continues to make public appearances and act in new films. She admits juggling the different duties is challenging but rewarding.

anxious when her older daughter was about two years old and Gadot had to travel from Israel to the United States for her work, speaking in English at work and Hebrew at home. She found herself feeling overwhelmed by the experience and struggling to be a working mom. But she worked through the problem. "It was my husband who told me: 'Gal, think about what kind of role model you want to be. If you want to show Alma that she can follow her dreams, that's what *you* should do, and we will figure out the logistics.'"[7]

> **"She's very, very proud... She already asked me if she can take over when I'm older."**

It seems that Gadot has worked out her child-rearing fears to a certain extent. In an interview with *E News* online, she stated that she tries to keep life as normal as possible for her children. "At the house I am the mother; I am not the star or the character or anything."[8]

But her girls do know what she does for a living. Gadot told *Glamour* magazine in 2017 that if her youngest daughter, Maya, is asked "Where's Mommy?" she'll cross her wrists and say, "Wonder Woman!" She knows enough about the character, joked Gadot, that she wondered if she was a princess because her mother was the on-screen princess Diana.[9]

Gadot's older daughter, Alma, on the other hand, has enough knowledge of her mother's work that she can imagine herself doing it one day. Gadot explained to *Entertainment Tonight Canada* that even though her daughter has not yet seen the movie, she understands what her mother does. "She didn't watch the movie yet," Gadot explained, "because I'm the mother and I just try to protect her and give her normal things, but she will definitely. She's very proud. She's very, very proud…She already asked me if she can take over when I'm older." [10]

A Role Model for Daughters

Gadot has thought about the roles available for women in the movies and feels grateful that the character of Diana Prince in *Wonder Woman* can provide a positive role model for her daughters. In an interview with *Entertainment Weekly,* she described a conversation she had with her oldest daughter, Alma, "She was saying something about the prince she saw in *Sleeping Beauty* and she was saying, '*He's* brave' and '*He's* strong,'"

Everyday Heroes

Gadot's work as a superhero has inspired many people, including other celebrities. In 2017, when Gadot found out that singer Kelly Clarkson's three-year-old daughter, River Rose, was a Wonder Woman fan, she sent the girl a package of presents. Her package included Wonder Woman figures and a signed photograph. Clarkson explained in an interview, "Once she saw the little girl in *Wonder Woman* defend herself and all that she loved, she started acting it out, and I couldn't have been more proud." Clarkson tweeted a thank-you note to the star, along with a photo of herself and her daughter with the package. [11]

Gadot has taken her job as Wonder Women seriously, using the part to inspire girls and women to be the heroes of their lives.

referring to the prince in the film, who wakes the sleeping princess at the end of the story. "And I said, 'What about the princess?' And she said, 'She's weak.'"

Trying to get her daughter to explain what she meant, Gadot asked her more questions. "And I said, 'What do you think of that?' And she's four, my daughter. And she said, 'She shouldn't be weak.' And I said, 'Why do you think she's weak?' And she said, 'She's sleeping the entire movie and the prince comes and kisses her and saves her. She didn't do anything.'"[12]

In comparison to the traditional princess story, Gadot feels that Wonder Woman has more to offer a young girl today in terms of a message. In an interview with *Glamour* magazine, she explained about her on-screen princess character, "She's not relying on a man, and she's not there because of a love story. She's not there to serve someone else."[13] She leaves her isolated island to use the powers she already has and ends up using her strength to help others.

Gadot purposely tries to inspire her own daughters with the roles she takes and tries to show them through example that they can also be strong leaders when they grow up.

CHAPTER EIGHT

On the Horizon

·························

G al Gadot's career has taken off exponentially since the release of *Wonder Woman*. Her future projects include not only *Wonder Woman 2*, but *Justice League Part 2* and a DC Extended Universe film called *Flashpoint*, about the superhero the Flash. She will also star with Bradley Cooper in a thriller called *Deeper*, about a former astronaut who sees supernatural events take place as his submersible vehicle reaches the deepest sections of the ocean.

A Fresh Start

Gadot's newfound fame allowed her to negotiate a better contract for *Wonder Woman 2* as well as a higher fee for other projects she chooses to work on. After working at an introductory rate for actors in the DC Extended Universe, Gadot proved herself and can demand higher pay for movies that she does in the future, competing with other actors.

Her negotiations for a better contract are not just to get more money, but for other things that she feels strongly about as well. For example, she voiced her concern about working with one of *Wonder Woman*'s producers, Brett Ratner, who had been accused of sexual harassment by other actresses who had worked with him on projects. One of those actresses was Ellen Page, who was directed by Ratner in the 2006 Marvel film *X-Men: The Last Stand*.[1] Others included Olivia Munn and Natasha Henstridge. Because Gadot had not yet signed

Gadot sits next to Lynda Carter at the UN Ambassador Ceremony at the United Nations in 2016. The actresses represented Wonder Woman as the character received an honorary ambassadorship.

a contract for the second installment in the Wonder Woman story, she had the power to take a stand about whom she did or did not wish to work with. With an increasing number of actresses expressing injustices that had been done against them during their careers, Gadot felt the opportunity to help the situation. She refused to sign her new contract if it meant having to work with Ratner. In a *Today Show* interview with Savannah Guthrie, Gadot explained that she was not the only one to not want to work with Ratner. "The truth is, there are so many people involved in making this movie, it's not just me, and they all echoed the same sentiments."[2]

Not only did Gadot get to negotiate her contract to avoid working with Ratner, but *Wonder Woman 2* was the first film to be produced with new anti–sexual harassment guidelines from the Producers Guild of America. The guidelines make an effort to prevent sexual harassment on film sets and in the film industry. A statement from the Producers Guild of American explains about the new guidelines,

> We are in a transitional moment as a society, in which we are re-evaluating behavior in the workplace and beyond. Producers possess authority both on and off the set, and can provide key leadership in creating and sustaining work environments that are built on mutual respect. Ultimately, prevention is the key to eliminating sexual harassment in the workplace. Through sufficient resources we can educate our members and their teams. Together we must model our commitment to a workplace free of harassment and encourage colleagues to do the same."[3]

Working Together for an Improved Environment

The topic of sexual harassment on Hollywood film sets was not just limited to producer Brett Ratner and his initial involvement in *Wonder Woman 2*. After sexual abuse claims and lawsuits against one of Hollywood's most famous and successful producers, Harvey Weinstein, there was an entire movement beginning in late 2017 to prevent such scandals, damaging behavior, and illegal activities from happening in the film industry in the future. The problem was so widespread that many Hollywood actresses and actors got involved in trying to help the situation and defend alleged victims in the media whenever needed.

Gadot did her part in navigating the difficult time in Hollywood as well. In October of 2017, soon after the news broke of Harvey Weinstein, Brett Ratner, and other powerful males in the industry, Gadot canceled an appearance at a dinner honoring Brett Ratner. At the premier of *Justice League* in November of 2017, Gadot and her costar Ben Affleck avoided speaking to the press to avoid questions about the Hollywood scandal. Avoiding press questions helped the actors keep the scandals from overshadowing the important event and the work done on the film by so many people.

Other people involved in the DC Extended Universe voiced their support for the action taken against sexual harassment and the outspokenness to support victims and prevent further problems in the future. The actress who plays Wonder Woman's mother, Hippolyta, voiced her support as well. Connie Nielsen stated to the *Hollywood Reporter* that she is proud to be part of a franchise that is so inspiring to young girls. She said that women and entire families can "all of a sudden show a whole different vision for their daughters' future."[4]

The Time's Up Movement

The anti–sexual harassment movement in Hollywood became so widespread that it spawned a movement called Time's Up. The movement was started by an alliance of female farmworkers who wrote an open letter to Hollywood actors to join with them to stop gender inequality and sexual abuse in the workplace. The letter was signed by hundreds of people in the film industry, including Gal Gadot. The letter was a call to action supported by the Legal Defense Fund. In just the first month since the letter of solidarity was introduced in January 2018, the Legal Defense fund raised over $20 million to help support victims of sexual harassment in the workplace and to support lower-income women who experience gender inequality in the form of unfair pay gaps for the same work.

The letter of solidarity between the farmworkers and Hollywood industry represented how widespread the problem is. The letter explained how the funds could be used to help victims. It read,

> Harassment too often persists because perpetrators and employers never face any consequences. This is often because survivors, particularly those working in low-wage industries, don't have the resources to fight back. As a first step towards helping women and men across the country seek justice, the signatories of this letter will be seeding a legal fund to help survivors of sexual assault and harassment across all industries challenge

Beginnings of the Time's Up Movement

The Time's Up movement that brought Hollywood actors and actresses together to fight gender inequality and sexual harassment started with an organization of female farmworkers in the United States and Mexico. The Alianza Nacional de Campesinas, which started in 2011, was designed to help female farmworkers and women in farmworking families get help with problems ranging from pay inequality, health care, and housing to sexual harassment or domestic abuse. A cofounder of the organization explained the reason for starting such an organization. Milly Treviño Sauceda explained, "So many of us had experienced sexual assault, harassment, reproductive health problems thanks to the pesticides we were doused in, unequal pay…We were all sick and tired of it."[6] Upon hearing of the sexual assault allegations in Hollywood, the organization wrote its January 1, 2018, letter titled "Dear Sisters" to the film industry as a gesture of solidarity and to show that the problems they face are widespread throughout many industries.

those responsible for the harm against them and give voice to their experiences."[7]

One of the things that Hollywood actresses did to support the Time's Up movement was wear black to the January 2018 Golden Globe Awards. Gadot attended the January 7, 2018, event and was interviewed about her involvement in the movement and how the story of Wonder Woman fits in to the efforts. She explained to *Entertainment Tonight,* "It means so much to me on so many different levels. I think that the movie really came out at a time when it was needed. And the timing and the story of this character and who she is and what she stands for is in an ironic way…really symbolizes everything that's really happening right now. So, I'm very, very proud to be part of this." As a tongue-in-cheek follow-up question, the interviewer asked if Gadot thought Wonder Woman would wear black to the event if she had attended. Gadot laughed and joked that the character definitely would wear black to support the Time's Up movement and that should would even carry a black lasso of truth.[7]

Representing Diversity

Many celebrities do advertising and endorse products for money. In January 2018, the cosmetics brand Revlon started a new advertising campaign to promote diversity in beauty. The makeup company's previous two ad campaigns had been about love. According to the company's press release, the newest campaign, "Live Boldly," is meant to celebrate the differences among women and to "inspire women to express themselves with passion, optimism, strength and style."[8] A company representative stated, "We are definitely shifting the way we communicate as

> "I think that the movie really came out at a time when it was needed."

At the 74th Annual Golden Globe Awards, Gadot joined many other women in wearing black to support the Time's Up Movement. Attendees also wore pins that said Time's Up to support the movement.

part of our 'Live Boldly' campaign and having a broader representation of women because we are a brand that represents women all around the world."[9]

Gadot was chosen to be a global brand ambassador for the campaign along with models Ashley Graham, Adwoa Aboah, Imaan Hammam, and Raquel Zimmermann. Each of the women has made her own statement about what she feels the campaign and "living boldly" means to her. Gadot was quoted on the website for the ad campaign as saying, "Live Boldly, to me, means owning it, being confident, being positive and going after whatever dream that you have."

The other women chosen for the campaign have overcome challenges in their lives and modeling careers, and they represent different ethnicities and backgrounds and have made efforts to be role models

Makeup vs. Feminism

As one of the global ambassadors of Revlon's Live Boldly ad campaign, Gadot has given thought to whether feminism has its place in a campaign designed to promote makeup. She told the *WWD* website in an interview that feminism can be considered "anything that makes you feel more confident, more beautiful and better about yourself. There's been a big misinterpretation about the way that people view the term of feminism. I have friends—girlfriends—who have careers and they're mothers and they do it all, and they are afraid to say that they're a feminist."[10]

The Revlon "Live Boldly" campaign includes Ashley Graham, Raquel Zimmerman, Gadot, Adwoa Aboah, and Imaan Hammam. The campaign celebrates the diversity of women.

and inspirations to others. Adwoa Aboah is a British fashion model who started an online community to support young women, especially those struggling with addiction and mental health issues.[11] American Ashley Graham was the first plus-size model to appear on the cover of the *Sports Illustrated* swimsuit issue and has been involved in many body-positive ad campaigns and has designed her own line of plus-size lingerie. Brazilian model Raquel Zimmerman and Dutch model

Since her first public appearances in 2009 for *Fast & Furious*, Gadot has been a rising star in Hollywood. Her attention to public issues helps make her a positive influence for many young people.

Imaan Hammam, of Arabic descent, add to the positive message of the campaign that promotes acceptance for women of different backgrounds.

"Revlon is such an iconic and groundbreaking brand, a champion of women, and I am so happy to be part of this family now," said Gadot in a press release from the brand. "There's a cultural shift happening, which Revlon celebrates, where feminine power is recognized, and I'm so proud that I get to witness and live this amazing change."[12]

Through the acting roles she chooses, the charity work to which she lends her support, and even the endorsements she chooses to take part in, Gal Gadot has shown the values that she wishes to portray to the public and to her family. Over the next few years, as Gadot continues to portray Wonder Woman on the big screen, the world will continue to get to know her.

Chronology

1985 April 30, Gal Gadot is born in Rosh HaAyin, Israel.

2004 Wins the Miss Israel beauty pageant.

2004 Is a contestant in the Miss Universe pageant.

2005 Enters Israeli Defense Forces for basic training.

2005 Begins serving as combat trainer for the Israeli Defense Forces.

2006 Meets Yaron Versano.

2007 Auditions for James Bond film *Quantum of Solace*.

2007 Begins acting in her first television role, on the Israeli television show *Bubot*.

2008 Marries Yaron Versano.

2009 Appears as a guest on *Entourage* and as a star in *The Beautiful Life: TBL* television series.

2009 Wins role as Gisele in the Fast and the Furious film franchise.

2011 Daughter Alma is born.

2013 The Fast and the Furious cast publicly honors castmate Paul Walker after his death.

2015 Trains for *Wonder Woman* role with DC Extended Universe costars.

2017 Daughter Maya is born.

2018 Supports Time's Up movement at Golden Globes awards ceremony.

2018 Becomes global ambassador for Revlon Live Boldly campaign.

Film Chronology

2009 *Fast & Furious*

2010 *Date Night*

2010 *Knight and Day*

2011 *Fast Five*

2013 *Fast & Furious 6*

2016 *Triple 9*

2016 *Batman v Superman: Dawn of Justice*

2016 *Criminal*

2016 *Keeping Up with the Joneses*

2017 *Wonder Woman*

2017 *Justice League*

2019 *Wonder Woman 2*

2019 *Justice League 2*

2020 *Flashpoint*

Chapter Notes

Chapter 1: Girlhood

1. Alex Morris, "Gal Gadot on Becoming Wonder Woman, the Biggest Action Hero of the Year," *Rolling Stone*, August 24, 2017, https://www.rollingstone.com/movies/features/wonder-woman-gal-gadot-on-becoming-badass-female-action-hero-w498704.

2. "Vital Statistics: Latest Population Statistics for Israel," www.jewishvirtuallibrary.org, http://www.jewishvirtuallibrary.org/latest-population-statistics-for-israel.

3. Marlow Stern, "Gal Gadot's Wonder Woman: A Hamas-Bashing, Ex-IDF Soldier and Former Miss Israel," Daily Beast, July 29, 2014, https://www.thedailybeast.com/gal-gadots-wonder-woman-a-hamas-bashing-ex-idf-soldier-and-former-miss-israel.

4. Holly Milea, "Gal Gadot Breaks into Hollywood's Major Leagues," *Elle*, November 6, 2017, http://www.elle.com/culture/celebrities/a13120963/gal-gadot-december-2017.

5. Morris, "Gal Gadot on Becoming Wonder Woman, the Biggest Action Hero of the Year."

6. "From Miss Israel to Wonder Woman: What You Need to Know About Gal Gadot," People.com, June 1, 2017,

http://people.com/movies/gal-gadot-what-to-know
-about-wonder-woman-from-batman-v-superman.

7. "Wonder Woman Gal Gadot Was Miss Israel in the Miss Universe 2004 Pageant," gmanetwork.com, June 6, 2017, http://www.gmanetwork.com/news/lifestyle /content/613486/wonder-woman-gal-gadot-was-miss -israel-in-the-miss-universe-2004-pageant/story.

8. Morris, "Gal Gadot on Becoming Wonder Woman, the Biggest Action Hero of the Year."

Chapter 2: To Protect, Serve, and Grow

1. Alex Morris, "Gal Gadot on Becoming Wonder Woman, the Biggest Action Hero of the Year," *Rolling Stone,* August 24, 2017, https://www.rollingstone .com/movies/features/wonder-woman-gal-gadot-on -becoming-badass-female-action-hero-w498704.

2. Philip Berk, "Gal Gadot's Military Training Helped Her Become Wonder Woman," thejakartapost.com, April 14, 2016, http://www.thejakartapost.com /life/2016/04/14/gal-gadots-military-training-helped -her-become-wonder-woman.html.

3. Ibid.

4. "IDF Background Information," mahal-idf-volunteers. org, https://www.mahal-idf-volunteers.org /information/background/content.htm.

5. Berk, "Gal Gadot's Military Training Helped Her Become Wonder Woman."

6. "The Chosen Ones: Israeli Defense Forces," Maxim. com, https://www.maxim.com/women/chosen-ones -israeli-defense-forces.

7. Ruth Graham, "Why So Many People Care That Wonder Woman Is Israeli," slate.com, http://www .slate.com/blogs/xx_factor/2017/06/01/why_so _many_people_care_that_wonder_woman_is_israeli .html.

8. "Gal Gadot Censored from Speaking About Lebanon 'Wonder Woman' ban," timesofisrael.com, June 1, 2017, https://www.timesofisrael.com/gal-gadot -censored-from-speaking-about-lebanon-wonder -woman-ban.

9. Ibid.

10. Nick Vivarelli, "'Wonder Woman' Banned in Lebanon Due to Israeli Lead Gal Gadot," Variety.com, May 31, 2017, http://variety.com/2017/film /global/wonder-woman-banned-lebanon-gal-gadot -israeli-1202448666/.

11. Ibid.

Chapter 3: Hollywood's New Gal

1. "Gal Gadot As Camille," mi6-hq.com, June 18, 2017, https://www.mi6-hq.com/sections/articles/qos -casting-gal-gadot-as-camille.

2. Corinne Heller, "Gal Gadot Thought She Was "Too Smart" to Be an Actress and Could Have Become a Bond Girl," eonline.com, April 12, 2017, http://www .eonline.com/news/843021/gal-gadot-thought-she -was-too-smart-to-be-an-actress-and-could-have -become-a-bond-girl.

3. Kirsten Acuna, "Gal Gadot Never Would Have Been Wonder Woman if She Wasn't Pressured into Trying Out to Be a Bond Girl," thisisinsider.com, http://www

.thisisinsider.com/gal-gadot-bond-audition-inspired -acting-career-2017-10.

4. "Gal Gadot," imdb.com, http://www.imdb.com/name /nm2933757/?ref_=nv_sr_1.

5. Holly Milea, "Gal Gadot Breaks Into Hollywood's Major Leagues," *Elle*, November 6, 2017, http://www .elle.com/culture/celebrities/a13120963/gal-gadot -december-2017.

6. Teddy Wayne, "Gal Gadot," Interviewmagazine.com, July 20, 2015, https://www.interviewmagazine.com /film/gal-gadot.

7. "Paul Walker: Biography," imdb.com, http://www .imdb.com/name/nm0908094/bio?ref_=nm_ov_bio _sm.

8. Julia Brucculieri, "'Fast And the Furious' Stars Pay Tribute to Paul Walker Two Years After His Death," Huffingtonpost.com, November 30, 2015, https:// www.huffingtonpost.com/entry /fast-and-furious-stars-tribute-paul-walker _us_565cbae3e4b072e9d1c2da31.

9. Brendan Morrow, "Gal Gadot Says She Still Hasn't Fully Processed Paul Walker's Death," cheatsheet.com, September 7, 2017, https://www.cheatsheet.com /entertainment/gal-gadot-processed-paul-walker -death.html/?a=viewall.

10. Derek Lawrence, "Fast & Furious Family Pays Tribute to Paul Walker on Anniversary of His Death," ew.com, November 30, 2017, http://ew.com /movies/2017/11/30/fast-furious-tribute-paul-walker -anniversary-death.

11. Adam Holmes, "How Gal Gadot Paid Homage to the Fast and Furious Franchise," cinemablend.com, https://www.cinemablend.com/news/1656560/how -gal-gadot-paid-homage-to-the-fast-and-furious -franchise.

12. Milea, "Gal Gadot Breaks into Hollywood's Major Leagues."

Chapter 4: Wonder Woman

1. "14 Things You (Probably) Don't Know About Gal Gadot," msn.com. https://www.msn.com/en-us /movies/gallery/14-things-you-probably-dont-know -about-gal-gadot/ss-BBBNnAL#image=12.

2. Dave Quinn, "Wonder Woman Gal Gadot Threw Her Back Out: 'I Tried to Save the World Once Again and It's Heavy Duty,'" People.com. May 27, 2017, http:// people.com/movies/gal-gadot-threw-back-out -wonder-woman.

3. Ibid.

4. Carrie Wittmer, "Everything You Need to Know About the Acclaimed Female Director Behind 'Wonder Woman,'" Businessinsider.com, June 4, 2017, http:// www.businessinsider.com/wonder-woman-director -patty-jenkins-2017-6/#but-jenkins-spent-the -majority-of-her-childhood-moving-from-place-to -place-because-her-dad-was-an-air-force-captain-she -lived-in-thailand-kansas-and-germany-2.

5. Belinda Luscombe, "The Short List: No. 7 Person of the Year 2017, Patty Jenkins." Time.com, http://time .com/time-person-of-the-year-2017-patty-jenkins -runner-up/.

6. Itay Segal, "Gal Gadot: I Often Stop and Say to Myself, 'Wow, It's Real.'" Ynetnews.com, June 3, 2017, https://www.ynetnews.com/articles/0,7340,L-4970098,00.html.

7. Ibid.

8. Nicole Sperling, "Wonder Woman: Gal Gadot interview."Ew.com, July 15, 2016, http://ew.com/article/2016/07/15/wonder-woman-gal-gadot-interview.

9. Ibid.

10. "Lynda Carter Biography," biography.com, https://www.biography.com/people/lynda-carter-10073461.

11. Ibid.

12. Brent Lang, "Gal Gadot Dishes on the New 'Wonder Woman' Film," Variety.com, October 11, 2016, https://variety.com/2016/film/news/gal-gadot-wonder-woman-dc-patty-jenkins-1201884362.

13. Mark Hughes, "'Wonder Woman' Is Officially The Highest-Grossing Superhero Origin Film," Forbes.com, November 2, 2017. https://www.forbes.com/sites/markhughes/2017/11/02/wonder-woman-is-officially-the-highest-grossing-superhero-origin-film/#73bfb6e7ebd9.

14. "Gal Gadot's Tight Wonder Woman Costume," msn.com, https://www.msn.com/en-us/entertainment/celebrity/gal-gadots-tight-wonder-woman-costume/ar-BBAPu4e.

15. Lang, "Gal Gadot Dishes on the New 'Wonder Woman' Film."

16. Jacqueline Andriakos, "Gal Gadot Responds to Critics Who Say Her Boobs Are Too Small for Wonder Woman Role," People.com, March 26, 2015, http://people.com/bodies/gal-gadot-responds-to -body-critics-on-role-as-wonder-woman-in-batman -v-superman.

Chapter 5: A Superhero Influence

1. Seth Kelly, "'Wonder Woman' Conquers the Domestic Box Office with Heroic $103.1 Million," Variety.com, June 4, 2017, http://variety.com/2017 /film/news/box-office-wonder-woman-opening -weekend-1202453353.

2. Nivea Serrao, "Wonder Woman: Gal Gadot Gets 'Chills' Reading List of Kids' Reactions to the Film," *Entertainment Weekly,* June 12, 2017, http://ew.com /movies/2017/06/12/wonder-woman-impact-patty -jenkins-gal-gadot.

3. Ibid.

4. Leah Cornish, "'Wonder Woman' Director Patty Jenkins on the Feminist Superhero: 'Being Badass Doesn't Mean She's Not Loving,'" Glamour.com, May 16, 2017, https://www.glamour.com/story/wonder -woman-director-patty-jenkins-on-the-feminist -superhero.

5. Ibid.

6. Michele Manelis, "Gal Gadot Says Becoming Wonder Woman Was an 'Out-of-Body Experience,'" *Herald Sun,* May 27, 2017, http://www.heraldsun.com.au /entertainment/movies/gal-gadot-says-becoming -wonder-woman-was-an-outofbody-experience /news-story/f210bf4d291a71fc8bab29449dd46437.

7. "Wonder Woman Star Gal Gadot Says It's 'Really Magical' to Inspire Youth with 'Strong Female Figure,'" ABC News, May 24, 2017, http://www.945bayfm .com/wonder-woman-star-gal-gadot-says-its-really -magical-to-inspire-youth-with-strong-female-figure.

8. Nicole Sperling, "Wonder Woman: Gal Gadot Interview," Ew.com, July 15, 2016, http://ew.com /article/2016/07/15/wonder-woman-gal-gadot -interview.

9. Krista Smith, "Cover Story: Brie Larson, Hollywood's Most Independent Young Star," Vanityfair.com, April 25, 2017, https://www.vanityfair.com /hollywood/2017/04/brie-larson-cover-story.

10. Brent Lang, "Gal Gadot Dishes on the New 'Wonder Woman' Film," Variety.com, October 11, 2016, https:// variety.com/2016/film/news/gal-gadot-wonder -woman-dc-patty-jenkins-1201884362/.

11. Sperling, "Wonder Woman: Gal Gadot Interview."

12. "'Wonder Woman' Star Gal Gadot Feels Responsibility of Being a Good Role Model," Today. com, November 19, 2017, https://www .today.com/video/-wonder-woman-star-gal -gadot-feels-responsibility-of-being-a-good-role -model-1099289667949.

13. Rachel McRady, "Gal Gadot and Patty Jenkins Talk 'Totally Different' 'Wonder Woman' Sequel," etonline, January 3, 2018, http://www.etonline.com/gal-gadot -and-patty-jenkins-talk-totally-different-wonder -woman-sequel-exclusive-93437.

14. "History At a Glance: Women in World War II," nationalww2museum.org, https://www

.nationalww2museum.org/students-teachers/student
-resources/research-starters/women-wwii.

15. Jill Lepore, "The Surprising Origin Story of Wonder
    Woman," Smithsonian.com, October 2014, https://
    www.smithsonianmag.com/arts-culture/origin-story
    -wonder-woman-180952710/.

16. Olivia Truffaut-Wong, "Does Wonder Woman Fight
    In Other Wars? Diana's WWII History Might Make
    for a Good Sequel," June 5, 2017, https://www.
    bustle.com/p/does-wonder-woman-fight-in-other
    -wars-dianas-wwii-history-might-make-for-a-good
    -sequel-62349.

17. Angelica Jade Bastien, "The Strange, Complicated,
    Feminist History of Wonder Woman's Origin Story,"
    Slate.com, June 12, 2017, http://www.slate.com
    /blogs/browbeat/2017/06/12/the_long_strange_and
    _uniquely_feminist_story_behind_wonder_woman
    .html.

Chapter 6: The Justice League's Best Gal

1. Mike Miller, "Justice League: Inside the Cast's
   'Chemistry'—and the Most 'Unforgettable' Moment
   from Set," People.com, November 17, 2017, http://
   people.com/movies/justice-league-inside-the-casts
   -chemistry-and-the-most-unforgettable-moment
   -from-set.

2. "'Wonder Woman' Star Gal Gadot Feels Responsibility
   of Being a Good Role Model," Today.com, November
   19th, 2017, https://www.today.com/video/-wonder
   -woman-star-gal-gadot-feels-responsibility-of-being
   -a-good-role-model-1099289667949.

3. "Gal Gadot—Full Interview 'Live With Kelly and Ryan,'" YouTube, Posted on November 15, 2017, https://www.youtube.com/watch?v=XgIeCTy86Bo.

4. Beth Elderkin, "Working on Justice League Made Gal Gadot Vomit Repeatedly," io9.com, November 16, 2017, https://io9.gizmodo.com/working-on-justice -league-made-gal-gadot-vomit-repeated-1820520144.

5. Warren Manager, "Wonder Woman Gal Gadot's Little Girl Had Secret Role in Film—but nobody noticed," Mirror.co.uk, June 6, 2017, https://www.mirror .co.uk/3am/celebrity-news/gal-gadot-says-born -play-10573332.

6. Mansoor Mithalwala, "Justice League's Final Box Office Is Much Lower Than Expected," screenrant. com, December 24, 2017, https://screenrant.com /justice-league-final-box-office.

7. Chris O'Falt, "'Justice League': Why Joss Whedon Is Only Receiving a Credit for Writing, not Directing," Indiewire.com, November 17, 2017, http://www .indiewire.com/2017/11/justice-league-joss -whedon-wga-screenplay-director-credit-33-percent -contribution-1201898421.

8. David J. Criblez, "LI Comic Con: 'Justice League' Cast Members Help Close 3-Day Event," Newsday.com, December 10, 2017, https://www.newsday.com /entertainment/movies/justice-league-comic-con -nassau-coliseum-1.15408272.

9. Brian Truitt, "Copy of 'Action Comics' No. 1 sells for $3.21 million." USAToday.com. August 24, 2014, https://www.usatoday.com/story/life/2014/08/24

/action-comics-no-1-most-expensive-comic
-book/14545215.

Chapter 7: Importance of Family

1. "Gal Gadot Is Wonder Woman: 'She Is Not Relying on a Man, and She's Not There Because of a Love Story,'" Glamour, March 7, 2016, https://www.glamour.com /story/gal-gadot-wonder-woman-cover-interview.

2. Ibid.

3. "Yaron Versano, 'Wonder Woman' Gal Gadot's Husband: 5 Fast Facts You Need to Know," Heavy. com, https://heavy.com/entertainment/2018/01 /yaron-versano-gal-gadot-husband-wonder-woman -married.

4. Ibid.

5. Warren Manger, "Wonder Woman Gal Gadot's Little Girl Had Secret Role in Film—but nobody noticed," Mirror.co.uk, June 6, 2017, https://www.mirror .co.uk/3am/celebrity-news/gal-gadot-says-born -play-10573332.

6. Sue Surkes, "Gal Gadot's Husband Shows Off Wondrous Wife," timesofisrael.com. June 19, 2017, https://www.timesofisrael.com/gal-gadots-husband -shows-off-wondrous-wife.

7. "Gal Gadot Is Wonder Woman: 'She Is Not Relying on a Man, and She's Not There Because of a Love Story.'"

8. Cydney Contreras, "Why Gal Gadot's Daughters Aren't Impressed with Her Wonder Woman Character," Eonline.com, November 6, 2017, http:// www.eonline.com/news/892033/why-gal-gadot

-s-daughters-aren-t-impressed-with-her-wonder
-woman-character.

9. "Gal Gadot Is Wonder Woman: 'She Is Not Relying on a Man, and She's Not There Because of a Love Story.'"

10. "Gal Gadot and Patty Jenkins Talk 'Totally Different' 'Wonder Woman' Sequel," Etcanada.com, January 3, 2018, https://etcanada.com/news/285481/gal-gadot -and-patty-jenkins-talk-totally-different-wonder -woman-sequel.

11. Alexia Fernandez, "Kelly Clarkson's Daughter River Receives Wonder Woman Gifts from Gal Gadot: 'She LOVES Them,'" People.com, November 28, 2017, http://people.com/babies/kelly-clarksons-daughter -river-receives-wonder-woman-gifts-from-gal-gadot.

12. Nicole Sperling, "Wonder Woman: Gal Gadot interview," Ew.com, July 15, 2016, http://ew.com /article/2016/07/15/wonder-woman-gal-gadot -interview.

13. "Gal Gadot Is Wonder Woman: 'She Is Not Relying on a Man, and She's Not There Because of a Love Story.'"

Chapter 8: On the Horizon

1. Christine D'Zurilla, "Ellen Page Says Brett Ratner Outed Her to 'X-Men: The Last Stand' Cast and Crew," Latimes.com, November 10, 2017, http://www .latimes.com/entertainment/la-et-entertainment-news -updates-ellen-page-brett-1510340425-htmlstory .html.

2. "Gal Gadot Talks About 'Justice League' and sexual harassment in Hollywood." Today.com, November 15,

2017, https://www.today.com/video/gal-gadot
-talks-about-justice-league-and-sexual-harassment
-in-hollywood-1096425539875.

3. Brian Gallagher, "Wonder Woman 2 Will Be First to
Use Anti-Sexual Harassment Guildelines," Movieweb.
com, January 22, 2018, https://movieweb.com
/wonder-woman-2-anti-sexual-harassment
-guidelines.

4. Aaron Couch, "Ben Affleck and Gal Gadot
Avoid Press at 'Justice League' Premiere,"
Hollywoodreporter.com, November 14, 2017, https://
www.hollywoodreporter.com/heat-vision
/justice-league-premiere-ben-affleck-gal-gadot-avoid
-press-1057621.

5. "Time's Up," https://www.timesupnow.com.

6. Raquel Reichard, "This Chicana Farmworker Won a
Global Human Rights Prize for Her Feminist Activism
on the Field," Latina.com, December 12, 2016, http://
www.latina.com/lifestyle/our-issues/chicana
-farmworker-won-prize-feminist-activism.

7. "Gal Gadot on What Wonder Woman Would Think
of the Times Up Movement," msn.com, January 8,
2018, https://www.msn.com/en-us/tv/recaps/gal
-gadot-on-what-wonder-woman-would-think-of-the
-times-up-movement/vp-BBI46Qk.

8. "Revlon Announces New Global Brand Ambassador
GAL GADOT," January 9, 2018, https://www
.prnewswire.com/news-releases/revlon-announces
-new-global-brand-ambassador-gal-gadot-300579982
.html.

9. Allison Collins, "Gal Gadot on Makeup, Feminism and a Cultural Shift in Hollywood," WWD.com, January 9, 2018, http://wwd.com/beauty-industry -news/beauty-features/gal-gadot-wonder-woman -revlon-makeup-feminism-hollywood-11084996.

10. Ibid.

11. Dara Prant, "Must Read: Adwoa Aboah's Rise from Model to Activist, LFW Met with an Influx of Fur Protestors." Fashionista.com, September 19, 2017, https://fashionista.com/2017/09/adwoa-aboah-model -activist.

12. Allison Collins, "Gal Gadot on Makeup, Feminism and a Cultural Shift in Hollywood."

Glossary

Allied powers Collaboration of nations that fought in World War II (United States, Britain, Soviet Union, France, China) against the Axis powers.

Ashkenazi Jewish people descended from eastern or central Europe.

Auschwitz Located in Poland, the largest concentration camp in use during World War II.

authentic Genuine; of traditional origin.

Axis powers Collaboration of nations that fought in World War II (Germany, Italy, Japan) against the Allied powers.

concentration camp A facility where large numbers of people were taken during World War II by German troops for hard labor or death.

ensemble A group of individuals that works together for a common goal.

feminism The support of women's rights issues and gender equality.

franchise A legal permission to make products related to a commercial venture.

heroine A woman admired for her courage or qualities; a female hero.

holocaust Death or slaughter on a large scale; the term

used to describe the systematic killing of more than six million Jews during World War II.

negotiate To plan, arrange, or discuss.

privilege A special right, rare opportunity, or honor.

proactive Controlling a situation before it occurs, rather than responding to it.

solidarity Unity or feeling of agreement between individuals or groups.

Further Reading

Books

Bergstrom, Signe. *Wonder Woman: Ambassador of Truth.* New York, NY: Harper Design, 2017.

Gosling, Sharon. *Wonder Woman: The Art and Making of the Film.* London, UK: Titan Books, 2017.

Sherman, Jill. *Gal Gadot: Soldier, Model, Wonder Woman.* New York, NY: Lerner Publishing Group, 2018.

Titan Books. *Justice League Official Collector's Edition.* London, UK: Titan Books, 2017.

Websites

DC Comics

https://www.dccomics.com

Official website of the publisher of Wonder Woman comics.

Wonder Woman: 75 Years of Heroics

https://www.dccomics.com/blog/2016/10/06/wonder
-woman-75-years-of-heroics

Tribute to seventy-fifth anniversary of the publication of the Wonder Woman comic.

Films

Justice League, dir. Zack Snyder, Warner Bros., 2017.

Keeping Up with the Jones, dir. Greg Mottola, 20th Century Fox, 2016.

Wonder Woman, dir. Patty Jenkins, Warner Bros., 2017.

Index